# Forty Weeks of Keeping Your Head Down

# Forty Weeks of Keeping Your Head Down

## A Chronicle of One Man's Journey from "Guy" to "Father"

Bill Bounds

iUniverse, Inc.

New York   Bloomington

Forty Weeks of Keeping Your Head Down
A Chronicle of One Man's Journey from "Guy" to "Father"

*iUniverse books may be ordered through booksellers or by contacting:*

*iUniverse
1663 Liberty Drive
Bloomington, IN 47403
www.iuniverse.com
1-800-Authors (1-800-288-4677)*

*Because of the dynamic nature of the Internet, any Web addresses or links contained in this book may have changed since publication and may no longer be valid. The views expressed in this work are solely those of the author and do not necessarily reflect the views of the publisher, and the publisher hereby disclaims any responsibility for them.*

*ISBN: 978-1-4502-0391-3 (pbk)
ISBN: 978-1-4502-0392-0 (ebook)*

*Printed in the United States of America*

*iUniverse rev. date: 4/8/2010*

# *Acknowledgements ...*

- This book was written on a Mac. This is not important to the story in any way, I just wanted it said.
- Book cover and Website design by Scott Mikolaitis. I owe you a case of the good stuff, my friend!
- Thanks to the good people at iUniverse for helping to make this readable. One thing I've learned from this whole experience is, just as soon as one gets to thinking they've got something really good and well done, have someone edit it.
- For input and advice related to this book, thanks to: The very few people I bothered about it in advance.

# Special thanks to ...

Mommy and baby: Obviously this couldn't have been written without both of you, but there's so much more to say than that. The light and spark you give my life is unmatched; you're the reason behind everything I do. Mommy, you have always been the reason I laugh and, for that matter, the reason I do just about anything. Thank you for our baby. (And thanks for letting me write this!) Quite simply, I love you. I cannot imagine anything significant in life without having you there to share it with. Fortunately, I see no reason for that to happen, so good to go!

Baby, you will someday know that you are the most amazing and wonderful thing I've ever been a part of. You will know how much I love you. I hope you will someday also realize how many people in this world love you and are excited that you're here with us. Until then, I'll just have to tell you every single day. You've only been with us a short time, but you've already got your pop completely wrapped around your tiny, pudgy finger. I cannot wait to start all the things we'll do together as you grow, but at the same time, I wish you could stay exactly as you are right now (only potty-trained).

My mom and dad: Love you guys. Glad we could give you a grandchild to buy "ruffly butt covers" for. Thank you guys for always being as supportive and helpful as you've been. I couldn't ask for more.

To Mommy's mom and dad: Love you guys too. I feel truly blessed to have married into this family!

To the rest of my family: What can I say but that I am absolutely the most blessed person in the world to have the family I do. I don't know how my brother Robert (who has the same sense of humor I do; sorry Christina!), my sister Shelly (who is ever so *Shelly-tastic!*), my mom, and I all managed to come through our youths even resembling adjusted and normal people, but we did (it's all just degrees of normal,

I suppose). As I'm the youngest, you guys had extra practice. Though I say it myself, I think you managed to make me just the right mix of normal and weird—interesting, but not criminally so. Thanks!

To all of my in-laws, to put it simply, you guys *rock!* From the first time I met you, you treated me as family, and I knew right then that I wanted to be part of this whole *thing* you've got going on. If I didn't know it would add twelve pages to tell you individually how special you are to me, I'd do it. Instead, I'll just say to all the Pastores, Kellys and Feolas, I love you guys! The love and support you've given us is amazing, and I am so lucky to have you in my life. *Viva la familia!*

For the unending advice, support and guidance during the entire period of time this book takes place, thanks to: Chrissi and Carsten Fritsch, Courtney Guerci, Eileen Enriquez, Kerry Lynn Lambert, all those who helped my wife but I may not have known it, my group at work, and all of our friends and colleagues that I haven't listed specifically. You know who you are … thank you! Apologies to anyone I've missed but it's been a long day.

To Bald-Eric Ihsen, Derek "D-man" Langham (FUD), Mark (nickname withheld to protect, well, me) Kulvinskas, Andrew "Big Mike" Wright, and Tawnya "Wubster" Graham: thanks for being … well, you know.

Bill

# Before I Get Started

The word "idiot" is tossed around pretty freely nowadays; This book will probably do so as well. Not to come across as arrogant, but I have always considered myself a fairly intelligent and well-adjusted individual who, for the most part, remains calm and gracefully works his way through any challenges that come up.

When my wife and I decided to start our family, however, I soon realized pregnancy was an area where I had a glaring lack of experience that, if not corrected, could be a problem for both (soon to be all three) of us. I suddenly realized I might just be an idiot—at least in this area. The more I started thinking about what challenges awaited us, the more I realized that it was quite possible I was not the only novice out there.

Fortunately, pregnancy, for all its frightening appearances, can typically be moved through with relative ease, provided one is properly initiated. As my wife and I travel along this road, I think that it might be helpful for me to document some of my thoughts and experiences so I can look back on them later and see what was running through my mind at the time. I also think others in my situation (meaning typical pregnancy-idiot guys) might be able to benefit from my experiences. Hopefully, my account of the pregnancy process will not only be entertaining but may also help others see the thought process behind my mistakes as well as my good ideas.

During a typical first pregnancy, at least one of the two soon-to-be-parents falls into the idiot category some of the time. It's time we came to terms with the fact that this role is most often, though not always, played by the man. Being a man, I feel I can admit this without having to hand in my man card. For this reason, many of the following pages are directed toward men; however, there is input here for women as well. At a minimum, women may find helpful insight into what men are experiencing and thinking during this critical time. So all you mothers-to-be reading this, don't shrug me off too quickly.

This book is designed to be an amusing and interesting documentation of my wife's and my experiences through an average pregnancy. This is not a how-to book. This is just what one man experiences and thinks about as he goes through it. Hopefully, sharing our experience will help other parents-in-training better prepare themselves.

For men, the journey from guy to parent is eerily similar to the journey from single to married. (Those of you out there who have taken that particular path will understand. Those who haven't are going to have to trust me.) In both cases, the man's job is to initiate the process and then stand back and make sure the woman involved is screamed at and hugged by her crying family when they are told the joyous news. He'll find himself immediately moved to the backburner, but his job is to come along for the ride and, along the way, be ready with the occasional "yes, dear."

Also in both cases, the man is often thrown a bone of responsibility to make him feel more "involved" in the preparations—but the truth is he's not. Men won't be, can't be, and, if they are honest with themselves, know that they don't really want to be overly involved. Once either of these rites of passage have begun, life for the male becomes a series of blurry shapes and forms whizzing by his head. Suddenly the big day is upon him; it happens so fast, he doesn't even have time to say, "Holy crap, already? But I just opened this beer!"

Of course, this does not mean the man is totally without genuine responsibility. One of the things I hope to do in the pages that follow is help the currently uninformed man arm himself sufficiently to move along this road as smoothly as possible (as smoothly as on any dirt road) and come through the end of the tunnel unscathed and maybe even—shudder—helpful. You're welcome, ladies.

We should not forget that, beyond the initiating of the process, the man is often without a clue as to what to do or, frankly, what he's really gotten himself into. Hopefully, through my account of these months of my life, we can all learn a thing or two.

While my primary purpose in writing this is to document these events in a hopefully entertaining way, keep in mind there will be times throughout when I give advice or guidance that may make me sound like, well, how do I put it? A pussy. While you, the reader, will probably never know me, you'll need to trust me when I say that it is not the case. I'm giving these nuggets—hoping to pass along some of my lessons learned as I go through these very things myself—just to help out a bit. Give a little something back, you know? Essentially what I'm saying here is, "Gimme a friggin' break!" There may be good stuff here. Read it, think about it, and, when appropriate, put it into practice. If you find it's not appropriate to take my tips, at least see if you can learn from my mistakes. Either way, you may thank me for it.

It should also be noted that this isn't what I do for a living. I am not a doctor, child psychologist, or author. I'm a software guy living in Silicon Valley, California. I don't suspect that I have answers you could not get elsewhere. So in those instances where I stray from documenting and enthralling to giving guidance, you owe me and any advice I give about the same respect you might give to a street bum you pass on the corner dolling out advice for a nickel. I am just an average Joe, observing and writing down random thoughts as my wife and I go through the process of creating offspring.

But that really is the point, I think. All those books that tell you what to or what not to expect, what to worry about, and what to be terrified of are written by people coming at it from any perspective *other* than that of the average Joe. (And I've never seen a pregnancy-related book that was intended for the male reader primarily, though there are almost certainly such books out there that I haven't come across.) I don't think I have some magical access to answers that others do not—although I have been told I "get" women pretty well, which, I will admit, helps as I go through this—but I have a point of view that is unique in that it's the same as everyone's, yet it's one that few write about. It's all about perspective.

As you read through this, I hope you will find relatively few places where I give actual, no-kidding advice. I don't really like to tell others how to live their lives. If something seems different from how you would do it or from what you think is right, then it probably is and you shouldn't do it—or at least not without serious consideration. You're an adult; make a decision and run with it. I have no responsibility for what you choose to employ, but I do hope that there may be some small bit of wisdom throughout these pages that helps you get through this entire show a little more gracefully.

I should also mention that some of the life lesson anecdotes are not from my own experience. Some of these are based on casual observations of people I know going through these situations or based on knowing how people—mainly guys—think about things. Likewise, not all of the challenges associated to surviving the female interaction part of this equation are from my own experience. Some of these are from times I've watched friends and colleagues get themselves into trouble with their significant others while pregnant. I'm very fortunate that my wife is not painfully neurotic, as it might appear if I didn't put this little blurb in. I'm not being entirely selfless in mentioning this point, of course; she's going to have to read this when I'm done and, hopefully, not kill me. Plus, our friends and family will also, hopefully, read this. I certainly can't have them thinking we're both nuts.

I will also quickly warn you that much of the first section of this book is not about the pregnancy itself, because we first had to, well, actually secure a pregnancy. This is to prevent my just listing out months saying, "Not pregnant yet." Instead it's filled with what a guy is thinking about—and is irritated by—as he starts to change his way of thinking towards becoming a father.

For the heck of it, I've decided not to use my wife's real name throughout this book. It's kind of a poetic license and just-because sort of thing. Also, it's to keep her from throwing things at me or quickly packing up and leaving after reading this. Anyway, my wife, for the purposes of this story, will be known as "Lucy." I've chosen this name because I don't believe there are any women out there under the age of fifty-five by the name of Lucy, which will help her feel confident I'm not writing this while thinking about someone else. Maybe I'm paranoid, but women seem to worry men do that sort of thing. Odd.

By the way, did you ever see those seasons of *ER* where they had that Lucy character? Man, that actress was cute. Really cute. I was bummed when they killed her off. If you haven't seen those episodes, you should. At least, check her out online.

# PART ONE

## Getting Knocked Up!

# 1

## *Getting the Whole Frustrating Process Started*

It's a wonder the human race has survived to become the dominant species on this planet. Seriously. Somehow an unfathomable percentage of teenage couples out for a nice, sweaty evening of backseat mambo walk away with an unwanted pregnancy. Yet when a couple actually *wants* to get pregnant, the chances of them being successful in anything resembling a reasonable length of time are just slightly above nil. There just has to be some medical conspiracy behind this designed to keep the OB/GYNs of the world in Porsches.

My wife and I have been trying for conception for fourteen months now without much luck. Well, that's not entirely correct: we've had luck—first good luck followed by bad. We were *very* fortunate that we didn't know about the good luck before finding out about the bad. Had we known, the emotional drain would've been considerably more taxing than it was, and it was already pretty bad.

Back to the topic at hand, though: fourteen months with nothing to tell the parents to get them off our backs has been an exercise in frustration. So many times the thought has crossed my mind to get the wife, drive over to my parents' house, park outside with a couple six-packs of Pabst, get her good and liquored up, and have a go at her in the backseat in an effort to try and fool our body chemistries into thinking we're seventeen and deathly afraid of successful fertilization. The only thing that's prevented the tryst, I think, is the fact it's an hour drive each way. I'm realizing now that the willingness to travel any meaningful distances solely for sex is inversely proportional to one's age. Certainly, when I was seventeen, I would've crab-walked backward to Uganda if I had even suspected it might impress a girl enough to let me round third base. Now, however, not so much. Plus, at two hours round trip, I'd feel obligated to go in and visit Mom and Pop just to make the drive more worthwhile. And let's be honest—going up and chatting with the parents after testing the car's shocks outside would just be creepy.

Men, this may be the first time during this process that you have a responsibility beyond the obvious. Take note: if you and your mommy-to-be have this sort of finicky conception cycle, it is 100 percent your responsibility to be there to support her and comfort her. If you ever hope to have non-purpose-driven sex again in your life, you will trust me on this. She is not being overly dramatic or too sensitive. This is a very difficult time for her; if you don't recognize that and support her, you may be a clinical idiot and beyond the help of the truly wise (such as myself).

There will come a time when she doesn't want to take any more pregnancy tests or even think about becoming pregnant. Trust me here: there is nothing you can say to make this better beyond, "We're going to get through this, and we will get pregnant; just hang in there." The moment you find yourself formulating a response beginning with, "Aw, honey, come on …" just shove a beer bottle in your cake hole, take a long drink, try very hard to look soulful and consoling, and think very carefully about the next words you say. If you can manage a tear, go for it. It may just save your life. Okay, it probably won't save your life, but it will at least save you an hour or more of trying to get her to stop cry-screaming at you.

By the way, don't think that the man completely escapes such frustrations. Certainly not. Honestly, basketball and poker playing guy though I am, I really want kids. I want to get the family started. I love kids. I'm really not all that fond of cleaning up feces or listening to the screaming, but I figure you have to take the bad with the good, right? Also, the clock is ticking for me. Granted, it's ticking differently than it is for my wife. I'm thirty-six now. If we get pregnant today, I'll be thirty-seven when the baby fairy comes knocking on our door (that's how it works, right?). At the rate we're going, I'll be heading right from my kid's high school graduation to my retirement party. At the little league games, cops will be asking why I'm hanging out around the bleachers. So yeah, it sucks for both of us, but I have to tell you that it's harder on the fairer sex. Us men, real men, need to understand this and be there for our ladies and, in doing so, help ourselves. This is my theory, and I'm sticking with it.

Also, truthfully, I hate seeing my wife this upset. I also hate when a family member calls and asks hopefully, "Any news yet?" I hate the subtle disappointment in their voices when I say no. Of course, when we finally do get to tell them something positive, it sure as hell won't be over the phone! Seriously, what are we, barbarians?

We recently started using more medical avenues to hurry things along, but even that has proven a frustrating process to date. We started off with just getting all the inner workings checked out. Hey, did you know that OB/GYNs' offices don't necessarily have specially outfitted rooms with scantily clad, superhot assistants to help a man secure his "specimen"? True story! In the case of Lucy's OB/GYN, there wasn't a room at all. I can think of nothing less reassuring to a man's masculinity than to stop at the doctor's office on the way to work and, knowing what's on deck, walk around the floor looking for a single-person bathroom while trying not to look like a sex predator. Of course, then there's the extremely helpful guy or cleaning lady trying to come in every forty-two seconds. "Someone in there?" Moment lost and, of course, it wasn't really there to begin with.

Ladies, you need to understand that, despite all you've heard to the contrary, most men are not on the prowl at all times looking for any opportunity to give themselves a solo run around the race track. Sure, *some* men are, but definitely not most. (A partial list of those who are can probably be found on the registered sex offender list.) This does not mean men don't think about sex much of the time, just that they're probably not merrily going through their days waiting for that opportune moment to duck into a closet and go to happy town. As a result, trying to secure a deposit for medical purposes in the public bathroom of a doctor's office with the pressure of a time limit can be somewhat challenging for your man, especially when the person involved has never had much practice securing it manually. Seriously, one has a better chance of getting aroused watching any Olympia Dukakis movie while doing advanced calculus than in this situation. So if you're forced to wait in the lobby of the doctor's office reading seven-month-old magazines for longer than you'd like, cut your man some slack.

Oh yeah, after he's secured his deposit, do him another favor and don't talk to him about it. The best thing you can say here is, "Are you going to the gym after work?" And don't get anywhere near asking, "Were you thinking about me?"

Over the past six to eight months, we've done a number of tests to make certain all is well with our respective plumbing systems. Apart from a need for me to switch to boxers, all is well. This is good news, obviously, but it adds to the element of frustration because we have no cause to hang our hats on, no answers for the delays. There are no quick fixes or silver bullets to make all right with the world. It's odd to find oneself hoping for something to be wrong simply so that it can be fixed, but that's where you end up.

On the topic of boxers, by the way, if you're a briefs kind of guy and you have to make the move to boxers for this process, do yourself a favor and don't complain to her about it. The woman in your life is voluntarily signing up to pass a large, screaming being out of a portion of her body that has only ever been treated kindly by you and her alike up to this point, turning that section of her anatomy into something a horror movie director would throw up looking at. Your switching to boxers isn't going to garner a ton of sympathy from her and will only make you sound like a whiny little baby by comparison. Suck it up.

# 2

## *Parenting Books and Web Sites*

We live in the world of the information superhighway. Unfortunately for most of us, the people responsible for putting up the signs along the side of the road are, more often than not, idiots. If you trust without questioning much of the content of Wikipedia or blogs when seeking guidance on dealing with pregnancy, you may be heading down a treacherous path.

There are libraries of books available to tell a parent-to-be what to expect, what to look for, what to try, and most intimidating, what to be afraid of. At least these books have been edited and proofread (theoretically), but if a parent-to-be, especially the mother-in-training, reads too many of these books or visits too many related Web sites, she may never open her front door again.

The truth is, the human race *has* survived to become the dominant species on this planet. And, I might add, it did so before the Internet and before any of the books, support groups, chat rooms or so on were available. I promise you that, if you try hard enough, for every book telling you to do something, you can find another book out there telling you that same something will be the death of you, your baby, and your baby's would-be high school friends. So what's the answer then? Good question. First, I think one key, really good book is needed to help you through the basics like what's happening to your lady physically during this time and how to prepare for that. But be careful about going overboard otherwise. On things beyond this first book, my advice is to find a source you can trust and basically ignore the rest. Just realize that no source is going to be the pregnancy gospel on every topic, and definitely not on the less obvious items. Parenting groups of likeminded folks can be a good place to start. The moment—and I do mean the *moment*—any source you are dealing with tells you something as an absolute do or don't (with the exception of anything involving recreational drugs, a coat hanger, or anything else not abundantly clear), throw it away. There simply are very few absolutes.

**Note**: The above missive does not apply to *this* book. Don't trust me on this? When you get a chance, check out one of the episodes of *I Love Lucy* where Lucy is pregnant with Little Ricky. She's smoking like a chimney *while pregnant*! Don't get me wrong, I don't believe one should smoke when pregnant, and I am not telling you to or that it's okay. And, yes, I would probably call anyone doing so an idiot, possibly even to their face. My point is, smoking while pregnant is a fairly commonly identified no-no today, but it wasn't really even a concern not too long ago. And, by the way, Little Ricky was fine. What I am saying is there are things you can do while pregnant that will guarantee problems with your child, and most of these things are obvious to anyone who can actually read this. For everything else, you can find a statistic somewhere that shows terrible things happening to a percentage (whether large or small) of the people who do it while pregnant, while someone else will tell you they think it's no problem. You will also run into friends and complete strangers who tell you they did some pregnancy taboo over and over and it was fine. Use your common sense here, folks; that's really what it boils down to.

Here are a few things to remember. (These lists aren't meant to be exhaustive, of course.)

- Some absolutes:
  o Coat hangers are right out.
  o So are recreational drugs; deal with it. With drugs, if you'd get arrested for simply having it, it doesn't belong anywhere near you, especially when you're pregnant.
  o Bare-knuckle boxing while pregnant is a bad idea.

- A few probably-best-to-keep-in-minds:
  o You're old enough to do what you want to yourself, but smoking really isn't good for your baby and you really shouldn't do it. I don't care how long you've been doing it or how much of your right it is—you can handle not

doing it for forty weeks. If you can't handle it, there's no way you can handle being a parent. Buy a healthy supply of birth control.

o You shouldn't drink either. I realize you may feel you *need* to, but maybe you should pick up some other vice during this time. Try chocolate.

o Everyone you know will tell you what to do, what not to do, and what never to do. Unless they have personal experience with these things, nod politely and walk away.

Most other things that are legal, and not blatantly obvious as don'ts, are up for at least some level of consideration, no matter how brief, based on your own belief systems.

I realize I'm being a bit flippant here. There are definitely plenty of dos and don'ts that aren't completely obvious, which these resources can help you identify. All I'm saying is to keep your head about you when you're consulting any particular resource and realize that not everything they say is the gospel.

Folks also turn to these books and resources to help them deal with the things that women feel or experience during pregnancy and to explore what may go wrong. Lucy and I are believers in two approaches here:

1. ***What does her body tell her?*** Human bodies are finicky machines. They tend to let their operators know if something is really, really wrong. Women should listen to their own bodies. When something seems strange or amiss in a significant way, check it out, but don't sweat the small stuff. Looking up every cramp, twitch, burp, or fart in a book or chat room can only lead to stress, frustration, and unnecessary worrying.

2. ***What does her doctor tell her?*** If Lucy's body is doing something that seems strange to her, she asks the doctor. If the OB/GYN says it's nothing to be worried about, we trust her on it and move on. No fuss, no muss. It's a nice approach. Her doctor doesn't mind the questions or the calls, so we don't mind asking.

And don't get me started on the pregnancy-related Internet chat rooms. Here, it's important to remember, are a bunch of folks who wouldn't be writing if their pregnancy had been a problem-free experience. Nobody goes out there and writes a blog on how beautiful their pregnancy was. Boring. No zip, no drama, no pop, no pizzazz. It would go like this:

- Month 1: No problem, everything normal. Threw up a lot.
- Month 2: No problem, everything normal. Threw up a lot.
- Month 3: No problem, everything normal. When the hell am I going to stop throwing up and be able to stay up for more than four hours without needing a nap?
- Month 4: Woo hoo! Not throwing up!

People have to understand that the authors are only going to share the horror stories. What one sees in these forums, therefore, is an extremely narrow slice of the population, but one where nearly all of the participants had some problem or another. It's easy for someone to read these accounts and think they are a true sampling of what women go through during pregnancy. From there, it's only one small step to thinking that it is what people should expect. Suddenly, any anomaly, no matter how small or insignificant, turns into a large-scale worry.

Climbing down off my soapbox for a moment, please note that I'm not saying these sources are without merit or benefit. On the contrary, I suspect they can be extremely beneficial, especially if this is your first child. And, regarding the chat rooms and so on, they can definitely be helpful if you know for a fact you are in a high-risk category. Having the experiences of other couples to check with and bond with in these situations can probably be a huge help. Again, I'm simply suggesting you take *any* stories, advice, or guidance—even mine—with a grain (or pound) of salt and realize that not all things that can happen, or have happened to someone else, will happen to you. And, if your lady isn't in a high-risk pregnancy category, she should definitely stay away from the chat-rooms and support groups for ladies who are. Reading their experiences and concerns will likely drive her nuts.

I realize you're very likely saying to yourself right now, "Easy for that guy to say all this; he's not even a parent or a parent-to-be yet." Well, you're right. However, I've done quite a bit of research and have discussed this topic with countless others who've survived pre-pregnancy and pregnancy, and all seem to be in agreement. We'll see, I suppose, how I feel about this topic later.

On the topic of doctors and asking questions, keep in mind that these folks work for you. You're paying them to be there. If you get one of those doctors who doesn't have time for your questions, whose style frustrates you, or who is frustrated by your style, find another doctor. The pregnancy is going to be challenging enough without the added stress of not trusting or liking your doctor. Don't be shy about asking questions if something doesn't feel right or is confusing. These folks aren't gods, aren't infallible, and aren't above answering questions to make you more comfortable. And you need to be comfortable with them. After all, you're trusting them to bring your child into the world!

The only book I can say is a near must-have in every parent's library is *The Poo Bomb* by Jeff Vogel. Sure, this book is more about what happens *after* your little bundle of grossness is born, but it's probably the best and most honest reflection of that time to come. Plus, it's more of a chronicle of one family's experience than a tell-you-how-to-do-it sort of book. It also has the added benefit of being hilarious. Pick it up, give it a read, and have a good laugh. Then be sad, for that will be your life at some point within the next forty weeks.

# 3

## *A Word on the Name*

Lucy and I have already decided what our first baby's name will be. Not sure how we have done so, considering we're not yet pregnant—that I know of—but we have. We decided early on not to tell anyone what the baby's name is going to be until all the papers are in and these details can't be changed without legal action.

I don't know why the general population of the world seems to feel the need to tell you what you should name your offspring. I don't get this tendency. Seriously, what would happen if I tried to tell someone what to name his or her dog? They'd get all pissy with me and tell me to do rude things to my mother. And yet it seems folks have no problem telling others what to name children. Odd. Save yourself the pain of having to listen to these people's opinions about your selection, and just keep your mouth shut about your choice until it's too late.

# 4

## *Another Word on the Name*

Don't be cruel. No matter how much significance or meaning a lame name holds in your heart or mind, it's still a lame name and will result in your child being ritually and repeatedly beaten during recess. I don't remember any child I grew up with being able to sufficiently explain the meaning behind his or her stupid name to the point that the bully about to kick their butt thought better of it. Kids have enough on their tiny little plates without having to start at a deficit of being named "Whisper" or "Grover." Stop it. It's not nearly as hip, cool, or meaningful as you think it is.

Having said that, I still think a name out of Shakespeare would result in a student-body president among my offspring. I'm still trying to convince Lucy this world needs a Mercutio and that we're just the couple to give it one. I think I've almost got her convinced. We'll all know by the end of the book.

# 5

## *Last Words on the Name …*
## *for Now*

I will share with you a theory I've been bandying around for a while now. Take notes—your kids' futures may be greatly benefited. If you want to practically guarantee yourself a future student-body president and/or captain of the football team, find a name for your child that has *Q* in it. Seriously. Don't make it a made-up name either—use a real name that you're spelling with a *Q*. It has to look cool when written too. Examples: Eriq, Marq, Toddq. Okay, maybe not that last one, but you get my point. I'm serious here, folks; I'm on to something. *Q*'s are the way to go if at all possible. You and your child, who for eight years of his or her life might just be called Mr. or Mrs. President, will thank me for it.

Also, definitely think about what their initials will end up being with the names you pick. Do your kids a favor and don't send them into the world with the initials DIK, ASS, or even less painful ones like PIE or MUD. Kids do pick up on that stuff, and really, if your kid is going to be beaten up at school, let it be because of something they did, not because of something you did to them.

Whatever you choose, keep in mind that some names may predestine their bearers to certain roles in life. Not all names—in fact, very few—but some, and even these not every time. So think about the possible indicators for a name before you select it and ask yourself if you're sending your child down a particular road before they're even old enough to know what a road is.

Just a couple of examples (certainly not an exhaustive list):

- A boy likely to end up being someone's stepfather: Brad
- Someone likely to be able to fix your car in a pinch: Joe
- A girl who just might end up being a newscaster: Melanie (though, she'll change the spelling to "Melynee" when she decides to become a newscaster)
- A boy who may end up being a washed-up, has-been rock-star, druggie douche bag: Axl

Of course, these are just tendencies I've noticed, not rules. So all you Joes out there that are rocket scientists, congratulations and don't get pissed off at me for suggesting you might have been naturally destined to be an auto mechanic. (And *please* don't think I believe there's anything wrong with being an auto mechanic, stepfather, or any other things listed, except maybe the druggie. Not so!) All I'm saying is, some names put one on a particular track and then it's up to the kid to jump to another.

# 6

## *Fifteen and Counting?*

I went to a friend's poker tournament tonight. I did okay despite having no playable cards for more than an hour. Getting blinded out was certainly more frustrating than just throwing money out the car window as I drove down the freeway, but at least it took longer. I got to spend more time with my money before it flew away from me. Plus, I did have the added benefit of not getting pulled over by a cop and having them ask, "Have you been drinking tonight, sir?" They never believe you. "Step out of the car, sir."

I went out in third place even though I hadn't played a hand in a round and a half and was generally really irritated about it. Turns out that my night was, at that very moment, as good as it was going to get. By a long shot.

I called home to let Lucy know I was on my way, something I tend to do. I could immediately tell something was wrong, so I asked, "What's the matter?"

"I started my period tonight."

Shit.

I have to admit, this month, I had foolishly lulled myself into thinking this would be *the* month. This had to be. Lucy actually got artificially inseminated. This just had to be the month. Clearly, from the tone of her voice, Lucy had pretty much thought the same. Racing home, I berated myself for stupidly thinking we were going to make it this month. I wasn't going to be disappointed any more, I'd said. Bullshit.

Getting home, I found a glimmer of hope. "It's not a normal period," Lucy explained. "It's very light and kind of brownish." (Yes, more information than any man should ever know about his wife's bodily functions.)

A light clicked on in my brain. I remembered her OB/GYN kind of perking up a bit when Lucy had told her that exact same thing a couple months ago. "Maybe," the doc had said, "you're pregnant right now. That sounds like implantation bleeding." It was shortly after that that we got the bad news I mentioned earlier. We *had* been pregnant and it *had* been implantation bleeding, but by then, we had lost the pregnancy. So maybe this wasn't bad news. Maybe we were pregnant and what she was seeing was just the implantation bleeding. We ran to the drug store and got a test. Doing the math in my head, even as we were going to the store, I knew there was really no way a test would come back positive even if we were pregnant, but I really needed us to check. We'd never have been able to sleep if we hadn't.

Negative. Shit anyway.

As I write this, I'm in a really bad mood. I know we have to wait another week or two to be sure it's another miss, but I'm really done getting my hopes up. I'm tired of flopping four to an open-ended straight flush and having it crap out on me. Anyone who doesn't play poker, trust me, it's pretty much the king of getting your hopes up to have them dashed like so much cheap glass. Now imagine fourteen months of that. We've been at this for so long now, and it feels like we're constantly playing the lottery. We keep at it and we keep checking the numbers, but no joy. Each time, despite all of our disappointments to date, somewhere in the backs of our minds we are already picking out colors for the nursery and figuring out how to tell our families. We're just like the lottery player who fakes nonchalance while checking the numbers while secretly picking out the model BMW he'll get. No matter how much we try to convince ourselves ahead of time we're not pregnant so we don't get our hopes up, we are still so disappointed.

As tough as this was for me tonight, this was far tougher for Lucy. Up until we started trying to get pregnant, Lucy had been telling me she was some sort of superfertile baby machine. She was clearly under the impression that she would get pregnant if someone simply threw sperm at her.

I had been joking all along that our not getting pregnant was, at least in Lucy's mind, somehow my fault. Suddenly, the jokes didn't seem so funny. Maybe it was somehow my issue, despite no problems showing up in the tests.

I really don't know anymore. I don't know anything except that I'm really, really disappointed.

In one of the early hands of the poker tournament tonight, I got quad-aces. Right now, I'd gladly give up every quad-aces in my future to find out next week that we actually are pregnant. Again, if you're not a poker player, that might not mean much to you, but poker players all over the world will read this and say, "Man, that guy is *really* bummed out!" They'd be right.

Right now, there's no really sufficient way to describe how I feel, so I will simply say, I am sad.

As for Lucy, she finally cried herself to sleep around 2:30 AM.

In around a week, I'll know if the months-disappointed clock is still ticking. Until then, I'm going to hit myself in the head with a tack hammer every time I think about us getting pregnant. If I'm lucky, I'll end up with some sort of Pavlovian response that prevents me from getting my hopes up in the future. Either that or I will be sufficiently concussed past the point of feeling disappointment, or anything else for that matter. I would be okay with that at this point.

# 7

## *Yep, It's Fifteen*

Well, it's confirmed: our oven is currently bun-free.

This news didn't come without some drama, however. For the next couple days, Lucy's monthly event was pretty much the same as it had been on poker night: lighter than usual and brownish, stringing our hopes along like a high school cheerleader being tutored by the president of the math club. But we weren't fooled completely this time. Neither of us was ready to dive back into the hope pool on this month's results.

Day three was different though. I went to lunch with several friends for one of their birthdays and was just about ready to head back to the office when my cell phone rang. I could see it was the wife.

Ever notice how, when you are in the worst possible position to handle inconvenience, inconvenience finds you? Well, not too long ago, I purchased a new cell phone. For some reason, it randomly freezes up when I try to answer calls. Clearly, this is a suboptimal response for a device whose primary function is to enable one to answer calls. It happens about 10 percent of the time. I went to answer the call, and naturally, it froze up. When Lucy was finally able to get me on the phone five minutes later, I realized how bad it was that this particular call was missed. It was clear by her tone that there was a problem. I asked, "What's wrong?"

"I'm bleeding all the sudden really, really bad. I need to go to the doctor right now."

Shit! Big time.

The first real emergency situation of this entire process appeared to be upon us.

Naturally, I hightailed it out and picked her up. She was calmer by the time I got there but was still very upset, as, of course, was I. We were both convinced this was another miscarriage. An afternoon at the OB/GYN and several not-fun-to-be-in-the-room-while-they're-happening tests later, we headed out, feeling better but still worried. Mercifully, the doctor called with the test results early the next morning instead of having us wait the entire day. We were, in fact, not pregnant this time at all. What Lucy had experienced was something very unusual but not wrong.

Of course, it was good news that we did not lose another pregnancy. That sucked out loud and neither of us was on deck for going through it again. It was also good because it meant we could try again immediately instead of having to wait a month or more for Lucy's hormone levels to normalize. So, all in all, no bad news beyond the usual—not being pregnant—so we felt much better today than a couple days ago.

Still, we were again so frustrated and really wanted to be done with this part of the process. I began to wonder how Lucy has been maintaining her sanity, but I started thinking I wouldn't be surprised if she cracked one day. I was starting to worry the contents of this book-to-be may someday be used as evidence in a trial. Time will tell.

Oh yeah, I want my friggin' quad-aces!

# 8

# *And, as Long as We're on the Subject*

Guys, honestly, going to the OB/GYN with your lady is just not that big a deal. So you have to sit in the lobby and read stale magazines for a while—so what? Maybe you even have to go in to the examination room with her. Again, I say, suck it up; it's not going to kill you, and it may earn you some valuable brownie points redeemable later for an extra night out playing poker with the guys or something. It's not like the doctor is going to say, "Hmm, Mr. So-and-so, the problem here might just be your plumbing. Why don't you have a seat up here and put your feet in these stirrups?" Then (holding up scary looking metal objects with hooks, clamps, and drill bits), "Good, now, you're going to feel a little pressure …" No really, you're safe. Besides, it's probably getting you out of work for a few hours in a way that no boss in his or her right mind would complain about.

It is odd, though, how much the word "sperm" is used in those offices. The word is sprinkled about like spice on a steak. I'm sure it's not odd for them—of course not—but for the casual, not-totally-mature male who is accustomed to that word being worthy of a snicker, it takes awhile to adjust to. Not unlike how female dogs are called bitches. Ever been to a dog breeder? I'm serious, it takes some getting used to how the word "bitch" is in every other sentence and is used affectionately to refer to these loving animals.

You do get to have some fun conversations when you're at the OB/GYN's. I'm sure they don't really appreciate all the humor (or attempts at it), but it amuses me and, after all, that's what really counts, right?

Two example conversations you might get to have (I have actually had both of these):
Doctor: "Okay, Bill, let's go through some basics here. Do you do any recreational drugs?"
Me: "Hey, I'm very serious about my drug taking. It's not at all recreational to me; it's more of a science really."
Doctor: "Yeah. Yeah, that's funny."

Or ...

Doctor: "... and when it's time to have sex, *no oral sex!*"
Me: "Look, Doc, I'm flattered, but really, I'm married. And, sheesh, my wife is sitting *right here* next to me! Man! I practically have to beat you ladies back with a stick!"
Doctor: Blank stare.

I've just decided here that I am tired of writing "OB/GYN." Therefore, this role will be referred heretofore as "GYNie" (pronounced: guy-nee).

# 9

## *Is It Possible to Simultaneously Projectile Vomit and Pass Out?*

Okay, I'm going to just come right out and state it for the record: I'm squeamish. Not Niles Crane–type squeamish but definitely squeamish. On a scale of one to ten (where a one is someone who can pop their own protruding bone back through the skin and stitch up the wound themselves sans painkiller and a ten is someone who passes out if they see a catsup stain on someone's shirt and think it just might be blood), I'm probably coming in around a six or seven. The mere thought of seeing certain things related to the human body grosses me out, let alone *actually* seeing them. For example, one day at lunch during my senior year in high school, the girl I was dating fell down some steps, did some type of flip thing in midair, and landed in such a way that she broke both of her legs in multiple places. (The Ukrainian judge dinged her for not sticking the landing or it would've been a perfect ten for sure.) I, being the dedicated boyfriend, ran over to see what was amiss. The moment I saw her legs (she was wearing shorts), with her feet pointing the wrong way relative to her shins, which were pointed in the wrong way relative to her knees, I nearly threw up all over her. The conversation went something like, "Oh my God, baby, are you okay—holy crap! I gotta go!" Then I turned and dashed away before she gained stains on her shirt to go with her disfigured and multicolored legs. You may think me a bad boyfriend, but I stand by my decision. I really didn't need to add to her woes by puking on her.

Since I'm so squeamish, certain words should just not be used around me in relation to bodily functions. For example, "crowning."

I don't want to know about anything that has anything to do with something on a person "crowning." Ick.

The wife and I have an ongoing discussion about my general proximity during the delivery of our offspring. If I have my way, I will be waiting out this potentially single-most-significant moment in our lives shooting hoops, playing poker, or possibly seeing Rush in concert. Heck, I'll even do the old-fashioned sitting in the hospital waiting room with the family. Given the near certainty that I will projectile vomit all over a sterile delivery room, I really feel this is doing everyone a favor.

Oddly, she has a differing view on the matter. She has informed me I will absolutely be in the room with her during this time and will be sharing this moment with her and the baby. I'm telling you, she's just not listening to reason here. I'll go in the room, but I cannot be held responsible for what comes out of me or what happens to things around me during the event. I've left it at, "I will be in the room if I can be completely covered in pillows so I don't crack my skull open when I pass out, with a feedbag strapped to my head to catch the flow of whatever may be flowing, horse blinders on my head to help me not see anything that should only be viewed by someone whose name starts with 'Doctor,' and my iPod in my ears cranking Rush, 311, Tool, or whatever will best prevent me from hearing words like 'crowning.'"

Again, don't think I'm being insensitive here. I'm actually being quite sensitive. Why turn this into a situation where we have a second patient in the room? That's all I'm saying.

Obviously, we have a lot of time before the blessed event to work this out. In the end, I'm fairly certain I will be in the room with her and the myriad medical types during the birth. She has generously capitulated and said I can, "stay up near the head." In truth, I'm really not going to be all that bothered about it, and I do believe it's important that I'm there. However, I will not be blamed for any puke or passing out. I have given fair warning.

We're definitely going to have someone filming the entire process. Not the actual birth; that's disgusting. Anyone who films these events then forces someone to watch them at dinner parties should be hit with something—and I would never even consider it. After all, I'm going to be spending the rest of my life trying to forget everything that happens in that room. Why the hell would I want video evidence to remind me? No, someone needs to be filming me and all that happens to me. This would be a certain fame-inducing Web gem here. Those guys lip-synching to whatever the hell boy band that was would have nothing on me.

As long as we're on the subject of things that make you vomit unrelentingly, Lucy is currently convinced she wants to do this thing called a water birth. Oh, this is a brilliant idea! You see, my wife is a clean freak. Just the idea of germs freaks her out. Heck, she won't even sit in a hot tub—an act she equates to sitting in a bowl of hot germ-soup. Yet, she wants to sit in a tub full of warm water, afterbirth, placenta, and who knows what other bodily deployments while squeezing out a screaming human? I think not! I'm just saying, there's a reason they put a bucket down there during deliveries. I sure as heck wouldn't want to bathe in it. I can see it now: "Congratulations, Lucy, it's a boy! Now, go hit the showers!"

Lucy, however, has heard that a water birth is a less jarring way for the baby to enter the world. My thinking is, eventually the baby is going to be taking its first shocking gulp of air one way or another; what's the difference if it's straight from the delivery portal or with a buffer zone of two feet of water? Zero. I'm certain that in her current image of this scenario, a water birth will ensure a calm and peaceful room where there will be harps playing and possibly little cartoon deer and birds fluttering about whistling tunes with her. The truth is, however, there definitely will be stress and it probably won't be calm and there might be lots of people running around, and it will be something entirely *not* peaceful.

I should add here that, up until just a hundred or so years ago, women gave birth standing up on wooden blocks. Their babies occasionally actually *landed on the ground*! I suppose they may have put a pillow or something down there, but the point is there wasn't much in the way of frills in those days, yet babies seemed to do okay.

In Lucy's defense, she's also heard—and this I do believe—that being in water during labor is considerably less painful. I can see that, definitely. However, medicine has afforded us a work-around for the absence of this water-related benefit; they call it an epidural.

By the way, in her scenario, Lucy is also not picturing me vomiting into the tub and everywhere else, but I can guarantee that addition to the equation if a water birth is involved. Vegas wouldn't even take bets on that one.

Fortunately, I believe this is something she will decide against in time through simple discussion with other folks. At some point, her friends, family, or GYNie will convince her that it's not for her, and I will never have to be the bad guy. I will never even need to have the discussion. I'm convinced of this. Oh God, I hope so.

# 10

## *Sure, Everyone Says Their Kids Won't Be That Way, but My Kids Really Won't!*

Ever been in a restaurant or store where some couple is with their child who is completely and totally out of control? You know, screaming holy terror and throwing things and basically making you wish for a heaping helping of Zoloft in their milk? Did you also notice how the nonparents or the not-yet-parents sit scowling at the family with a holier-than-thou look that says, "My kid will *not* act that way"?

People judge situations like this all the time. My wife and I do it too. It's an illogical and silly response, of course, as it implies either that there is something the parents aren't doing to correct the behavior but could be if they wanted to or that they somehow just didn't notice.

The truth is the parents can't do anything about it and they absolutely do notice. Well, they probably *can* do something about it but only in ways that might get them arrested if done in public. Kids, when they get to the "let me see how much I can annoy anyone within earshot" age, are all about asserting independence while, ironically, craving attention from their parents, or if they're like I was, absolutely anyone. So when the kids are screaming and throwing things and the parents are ignoring it, I'm convinced it's a defense mechanism for the parents. They know that showing that child even a modicum of attention only reinforces their behavior, and therefore, delays the overall goal of slowly breaking that child's will.

They also know a secret the average nonparent doesn't know, but I have discovered and I'm willing to share with you here: Eventually, if ignored, the temper-tantrum-throwing children will become aware this strategy is not garnering them the attention they so desperately crave and will grow tired of making the fuss. They will calm down out of sheer boredom. (Well, I like to call it lack of follow-through and stick-to-it-iveness.) A screaming child will eventually calm down much for the same reason, but also because it takes a tremendous amount of energy to scream so loud and for so long. So what if the innocent passersby or fellow restaurant patrons are forced to witness the conniption for as long as it takes the child to bend? The parents have to live with it all the time; what do they care if someone else gets it for ten minutes?

Case in point: One of my colleagues from the East Coast, who I have always felt was an exceptional mother to her kids, was recently visiting us with her husband and two kids. I took her, her four-year-old little girl, and her not-quite-two-year-old little boy out to lunch. As soon as we sat down, the boy began looking for things on the table to play with, throw, break or smash. If his fidgeting garnered him any attention at all from either us at the table or anyone at another table, he would instantly ratchet up the noise making to a genuine ruckus. Eventually, my colleague would, without breaking conversational stride or acknowledging the child at all, quickly reach over, take from him whatever item he was fussing with and move it out of his reach. The boy would just stop and stare blankly at his empty hands for a moment and wonder how the thing he had been holding just seconds prior had disappeared from his grasp. He seemed to figure he had somehow just missed something and would then move on to the next thing, and the process would repeat. At one point, I bent down to pick up a spoon he dropped. My colleague said, "No no, leave it. He needs to understand that when he drops something, he loses it."

It was too late though; I was too quick and had grabbed the spoon and handed it to the boy. Immediately, he knew he had me. The realization dawned upon his face as surely as if he had just said, "You're mine, bitch." From that moment on, he was banging, throwing, screaming, or tearing absolutely anything and violently rocking the high-chair he was sitting in. Eventually, we'd sufficiently ignored him to the point that he calmed down, but it took ten minutes with people at every other table shooting us nasty looks.

The little girl literally said to me, "Bet you won't do that again, huh?"

So the next time you're witnessing such a display at the next table or in the store, keep in mind all may not be as it appears. These really may be exceptional parents who have realized there are moments they can't control. Or they may be formerly exceptional parents who have lost the will to live entirely. Of course, these could also be lousy parents with lousy kids, but you're not likely to ever know them well enough to find out for sure, so best to give them the benefit of the doubt.

I will say, however, that some of the things one witnesses in other people's kids just don't make sense and, if it kills me, my kids will not do. For example, when did we, as a society, stop telling our kids to chew their food with their mouths closed? I just can't believe how often I see families in restaurants with kids chewing away on their cud, mouths lolling open like some kind of poorly dressed adolescent cow, and the parents just sitting there talking with them as though seeing half-masticated waffles was exactly what they needed to get their Sundays started on the right foot. Do people not realize how disgusting this looks or how single-digit-IQ it makes them appear? To this day I can vividly recall my mother needling me if she caught me chewing with my mouth open or talking with my mouth full. Back then, I'm certain I made quite the production of rolling my eyes in response, but now I can quite honestly say, "Thanks, Mom! People aren't ashamed to be seen with me in public. Good on ya!"

Similarly, Lucy and I were in a restaurant not too long ago where four families were all eating together at another table. Actually, a better way to put that would be to say the parents were eating and doing their level best to forget they had children. The result was that nine kids were running around a restaurant—a real, sit-down Italian restaurant, not fast food—playing tag and singing songs in unison at the top of their voices and screaming at each other. (True story!) The parents, in some sort of twisted exaggeration of the "ignore it and they'll get tired of it" approach, sat there and drank their wine, feigning obliviousness to the suffering of the other patrons and the staff of the restaurant. In this situation, I did not blame the children. The kids weren't born this way; they were made this way. This was just a textbook example of really, really bad parenting. Each and every one of the adults in question should've been hit with something, preferably a truck. By the way, the restaurant was in Mountain View, California. If any of the parents in question happen to be reading this—and you know who you are—you suck!

I know saying this makes me seem like one of those "I had to walk to school ten miles, uphill, waist deep in snow" kind of people, but this sort of behavior, when I was a kid, would not have been tolerated by my parents or the restaurant or the people at the other tables. What's worse, if I or anyone else had gone up to these parents and asked them to actually act like parents, they probably would've gotten all high and mighty and freak out telling me I can't tell them how to raise their children, and I would've been the bad guy! When did this become acceptable? When did apathy about common courtesy to others become in vogue? It sucks and should be illegal, but folks are so worried about getting sued nowadays that nobody's willing to say anything about anything to anyone. Sad. Really sad.

No kidding here, my kids will not act this way if I have to strap their right wrists to their left ankles anytime we're in public to prevent it.

# 11

# *Speaking of Environmentally Engineering Your Kids*

My sister-in-law wanted her kids to be right-handed. In fact, she was determined that her children were going to be right-handed. If she saw either of her daughters favoring the left hand while playing with something or reaching for something, she casually took the item and placed it in the right hand. This is not, in any way, a criticism and is, in fact, understandable.

I think the benefits of being left-handed are under-thought, however. If there's a way to ensure my kids end up left-handed, I'm going to seriously consider it. Look at pretty much any professional sport nowadays; lefties are a hot commodity in every one of them! Basketball? Absolutely. Baseball? You know it! Tennis? Oh yeah. Golf? Well, not so much. So, basically, if you want to do all you can to ensure living vicariously through your NBA all-star point guard son, make sure he's a southpaw. If you long to hear your son dedicate his Cy-Young Award acceptance speech to you, find a way to make him a lefty. Want your little girl to break records at Wimbledon? Get her working on that left-hand backhand return. This is such an advantage in sports, it's incalculable.

How many times do you hear, "Steve Nash finishes it off with a beautiful left-handed runner!"? Then there's Steve Young; left-handed Super Bowl quarterback! (By the way, Steve Nash isn't left handed; it's just that he can dribble and shoot extremely well as a lefty. Still, my point is valid.)

There's just no question that dirty shirtsleeves and backward slanted handwriting is worth the fame and fortune that awaits you—er, I mean them.

# 12

## *It Must Be Something in the Water. Can We Get a Sip, Please?*

Month sixteen is upon us and we begin again. If we're both lucky—meaning the author and reader—there will be good news to end this month with.

So many people we know right now are expecting. It really has to be something in the water. My brother and his wife are expecting their third, and two of our closest friends residing in Germany are expecting their first. Lucy and I don't begrudge any of them their happiness and are not in the least bit bitter about their successes where we have had none. Honestly. My brother's two little girls are beautiful, and I couldn't be happier about the pending third. Our friends in Germany are just terrific, and they're as eager for us to have kids as we are. So envy? Maybe. Bitterness? No.

Then there's walking through my office building and corporate campus. There are so many pregnant women around campus right now that, if they all delivered within a month of each other, the company might not survive. The dip in productivity could be catastrophic. We would have to say something about it in our earnings announcement. Once again, I'm not bitter here—well, when it comes to people I don't know, maybe I'm a little bitter—, but not much! —but it does cause one to wonder what's happening with all the baby producing right now that somehow Lucy and I are out of touch with.

I stopped by a colleague's desk earlier this week, and coincidentally, his mother was there with his five-month-old daughter. (Had I known he'd recently had a baby, I might not have stopped by.) This little girl was, and I'm not exaggerating here, absolutely perfect. Big blue eyes, dimples—oh yeah, she was working the entire cute-baby package. When she saw me, she gave me this shy, sheepish little smile and literally batted her eyelids. It was almost painful.

Obviously, there's nothing to do about this but try not to let it affect my general demeanor. I consider myself a rather gregarious person and fairly approachable all around, so I'd hate to let a little thing like other people's success where I have not yet had any cause me to lose my reputation. I can see it now: I'll be sitting in my office one day and some lady I don't even know who's about ready to go into labor will come in to ask me a question, and, without thinking, I'll say, "What do you want, *breeder*?"

Lucy and I are in our second month of trying Clomid to regulate her various internal workings. A colleague of mine with two kids swears by the stuff. She's been through it before, so I value her judgment in the matter. On either Monday or Tuesday of next week, we'll be going in for our second attempt at forced insemination. So, in anticipation of that ever-so-fun trip to the GYNie, I've been trying to figure out if it really is something in the water for all these women so I can surreptitiously slip it into Lucy's drinks. I'm still working on it, but I think I've got a bead on it: these pregnant women all seem to go to the bathroom inordinately frequently. It just can't be coincidence.

On the topic of other women being pregnant, a word of advice to all the men out there: be extremely careful when asking a woman anything at all about her pregnancy. Unless you are 100 percent certain that woman is pregnant, it's probably best to keep your mouth shut. There's nothing in the world worse than being wrong about something like that. I've seen it happen, and it wasn't pretty. In a restaurant once, a woman asked the hostess, "Oh, how exciting for you; when are you due?"

Response: "I'm not pregnant."

Silence.

I thought the lady that asked the question was going to slit her own wrists or possibly lob a hand grenade just to break the tension. Man, it was so uncomfortable; I was in pain along with both of them.

My general operating principle here is, unless the woman in question proactively volunteers that she's pregnant in clear and unmistakable terms, I keep my mouth shut. There has to be no question about her meaning. Something like:

Woman: "Man, I can't wait to get this kid out of me!"

Me: "Oh, really, you're pregnant? I had no idea!"

Woman: "Don't be stupid. I'm eight months pregnant."

Me: "Well, you carry it exceptionally well. I am shocked."

If a woman starts a conversation with, "Man, I sure hope I have a son," be careful; it could be a trap. She could be speaking about her far-off future plans, and you don't want to have to spend the next hour of your life prying your foot out of the back of your throat.

For me, if I don't have clear prior warning that a woman I know is pregnant and I somehow come across her being wheeled into a maternity delivery room on a gurney, screaming in pain, with doctors all around talking about her being dilated, I might venture a, "Hey so-and-so, what's going on? You okay?" Even this approach, however, I consider risky.

Practice looking surprised, too, guys. It can be quite helpful. Even if you're certain a woman you're talking with is pregnant, flashing that look of surprise when she tells you is a handy way to make her day and put you on her good side. And really, there's just nothing wrong with getting on a hormonal woman's good side whenever you get the chance. It's much better than the alternative.

# 13

## *Fun with Turkey Basters*

Our second artificial insemination is now complete. With any luck, we'll soon have our oven full of buns. I will refrain from adding comments here about how significantly our luck would have to change for this to happen. I am, once again, endeavoring not to get my hopes too high. Lucy says she's doing the same, but I'm already hearing comments like, "Hmmm, my breasts are getting sore! Could be ..." with an excited look on her face. I realize she's only joking, but there definitely is an element of hopeful delusion here as well. I try to help by telling her it is way too early for such pregnancy-related symptoms to be evident and that any soreness in her breasts is there only because I've been flicking her in the nipples as she sleeps. Sure, this response has caused her to shoot nasty looks my way, but I feel it's worth it if I can save a little frustration later.

Near as I can tell, I have about two weeks to come up with a way to talk her off a ledge in case this attempt also fails. I'm not certain, however, who will be talking me off *my* ledge. A bridge I shall cross—or not—when I come to it, I suppose.

With this attempt at insemination, we were forward-thinking enough to plan things out so that I didn't have a repeat of last month's bathroom follies. Amazing, the difference. All we really needed to do was ensure that the trip to the GYNie's could be made in less than thirty minutes. Planning the most direct and most time-efficient route was the key. It was a risky move, of course, because traffic in Silicon Valley is not quite as predictable as earthquakes, but Lucy made it with time to spare. So, once again, we started the wait. I quickly decided that if I got no quad-aces poker hands in the next two weeks of our home poker games, it's a sure sign we made it. What else could it possibly be? On a totally unrelated matter, driving to work the other day, I was passed by a woman driving a rather pricey car outfitted with the following two bumper stickers:

1. My child is on the honor roll at Such-and-Such elementary school

2. Don't drink and drive, you might spill your drink!

I already have an opinion that bumper stickers are ridiculous and insipid, especially on a car valued in excess of $50K, but add to it how completely stupid these particular ones are in concert, and I'm at a loss for what to think. First of all, anyone who is sporting one of those honor roll stickers is a braggart. I am also convinced they're putting a huge amount of pressure on their child. Seriously, those things are *permanent!* They just won't come off without taking all the paint with them, so what happens if little Bobby Jr. has a tough year and suddenly takes a dip in grades? Keeping that GPA up for the sake of the bumper sticker could be just the extra stress that sends him right over the edge. "Bobby, you gotta pick up those grades. See that bumper sticker? You wouldn't want to make a liar out of Daddy now, would you?"

If you're determined to put those stickers on your car, I think scotch tape is the way to go. You may think me insensitive here, but this could preserve the car's overall look and also provide a little extra motivation for junior. So, it could be saving your resale value as well as propelling them to academic stardom. "I'm sorry, Bobby, you didn't quite make the cut this semester. We'll see if we can't put this back on the bumper after next. I notice Timmy's dad still has a sticker on his car. Hmm, I really envy Timmy's dad. You better get to studying." We're talking valedictorian for sure.

And then there's that second sticker. Seriously, even upon first read, this particular sticker has the peak comedic value of a box of wet sand, yet this woman gets such a kick out of it that she defiles a perfectly good BMW for it. I can picture her first seeing this on the rack of stickers at her local tobacco shop, laughing hysterically, and slapping down the seventy-five cents for it while wiping away tears.

Then, she saunters merrily home, wets down a paper towel, wipes clean the perfect spot to ensure proper sticking of this work of bumper-art, and slaps it home. After minutes of admiring it from ten steps back, she just has to take the car for a drive, confident that everyone behind her is praising her comedic genius.

And, really, what does it say about the home life in that house when one brags about her kids and her love of drink at the same time? I don't know, I just think this is somehow odd.

I do realize I am being too hard on this woman. I'm certain one of these is a joke, and she probably just has it for a little chuckle, not caring how far below market value the simple act of affixing this bumper poetry has plummeted her car. Maybe it's an inside joke of sorts that her friends all chuckle at as well. I mean, it has to be a joke—no way she has a kid on the honor roll.

On yet another unrelated note, Lucy and I went to a party yesterday. It was a party my boss was throwing, so it was a fairly adult crowd with lots of intelligent conversation and good food. One of my team members brought his family, including his three-year-old daughter, who, like some sort of toddler-succubus, immediately recognized our struggles and latched on to Lucy as if wanting to zap us of our collective will to live. Lucy spent most of the party playing with the little girl, who was, admittedly, adorable. Naturally, this caused the ride home to be full of, "I really want a baby."

Of course, at the party the mother provided the obligatory, "Want her? You can have her cheap!" We politely chuckled. I was worried for a moment when I thought I saw a look of *"Deal!"* in Lucy's eyes, but all was well and we did not have any embarrassing incidents as we left. Turns out, you can't buy a baby from someone. It's against the law. I checked.

# 14

## *Ding, Ding, Ding, We Have a Winner!*

Month sixteen came and went without significant event. As I mentioned, once again, Lucy did the Clomid and we did the artificial insemination thing. The end of the month came along in much the same way so many others before had: negative. Fortunately for our sanity, however, this time we really had managed to keep our wits about us and not get our hopes up. Well, not as much. It was a disappointment, of course, but our survival instincts had kicked in, and we managed not to be overly surprised or disappointed.

Month seventeen arrived on our calendars with a "let's reset" way of looking at it. Lucy was fine to do the Clomid again, but we decided against the artificial insemination this time, opting instead to go back to the more traditional way of securing pregnancy. We both agreed we needed to take a bit of the science out of it for a month or two and, along with it, some of the pressure we'd been piling on ourselves.

So for the days leading up to her fertility monitor showing it was time to get busy, we began getting to work every other day and continued doing so until a few days after the monitor had indicated the window had closed so we were either through it or not. For the remainder of the month, we didn't really discuss pregnancy in any meaningful way. And not in that elephant-in-the-room sort of way of not talking about it, but just really not discussing it.

Over the week or so that Lucy would normally be expecting to see the first signs of a negative result, she saw none. Instead, I heard her once again saying things like, "My breasts are getting sore ..." or "I'm feeling nauseous …" Being the good husband I am, I again reverted to downplaying these things in an effort to keep her from getting her hopes up. It was clear that there was something different about this month though. For example, there was the terrific argument in the car about our dog, and uh, something else, I think, that resulted in her crying hysterically and my not saying another word for over an hour. Good times.

Finally, on Monday we agreed she would take a test that coming Saturday, which was about as early as we could expect a positive result to show. For the next couple days, however, more comments about her breasts or nausea came up, so we agreed she'd take the test before work on Thursday. My thinking was, if it's going to be negative again, the sooner we learn it, the better. The excuse Lucy used was that she had an appointment with an acupuncturist on Friday to discuss whether fertility assistance might help us. If she was going to cancel the appointment, she'd need to do it on Thursday.

As I got out of the shower Thursday morning, Lucy, waiting for me with a smile on her face, yelled, "*Positive!*" It was a terrific moment for the obvious reason, but add to it that it suddenly ended such a long period of frustration and negativity. It was as though someone had opened a window and all that stress just flew out. Lucy, of course, explained that she had been sure of it for the entire week. "There were so many indications," she said, "like my mood swing in the car that night!"

Yeah, sure, that's what that was—a friggin' mood swing. Nifty. Why don't men ever get to wipe slates clean by saying something they did was the result of a mood swing? Where's our get-out-of-jail-free mood swing card?

We were, obviously, ecstatic. Barring an emotionally devastating problem coming up (fingers crossed, knock on wood, and all that crap), all the waiting and frustration was instantly behind us.

In the end, it was a little bit of science and a lot of good old hard work and elbow grease that got the deed done. I know it wasn't really hard work and elbow grease, but it was, as so many people told us, getting the stress and "effort" out of the equation that, I'm convinced, helped us turn the corner. We were elated.

Now all we have to do is get through to Christmas before we tell anyone. No idea how we're going to do that because it just isn't within

Lucy's power to *not* tell someone exciting news. This could be a huge issue because we're going to be spending a week with her family over Thanksgiving. These are great people, by the way, and I love them. I would love nothing more that to tell them our great news and brighten their holiday too, but after the problems we had before, I'm really hoping we can keep it a secret until we're back out there for Christmas and through the danger period. I think we can do it. I may have to duct tape a gym sock in Lucy's mouth to accomplish it, but I'll do whatever is necessary in the name of family happiness. I'm a giver, you see.

The past few days have been great. Lucy and I are both on cloud nine, neither able to focus on work for more than thirty seconds before drifting off to thoughts of what the baby's room should look like. As for me, I've already picked out the Phoenix Suns booties for the baby to wear. I'm certain that the elation of the news is clouding our minds and not letting us focus yet on the life-altering events that have been set in motion. All things related to getting across the baby finish line are ahead of us, and we've only just left the gate. There are thirty-six more weeks of challenges ahead, to be followed by a lifetime of illnesses and worry but also happiness and joy. The idea of watching my baby laugh for the first time or take its first steps is almost overwhelming, and the baby's not even here yet. Heck, the baby's not even out of zygote stage yet.

Last night, by the way, I won a huge pot with quad fives. Not quite quad aces, but I'll take it and consider all things even.

Now, if you'll excuse me, I have to go into the other room and throw up.

# PART TWO

## The First Three Months: Cool, Look How Many Different Things You Have to Worry About!

# 15

## *Okay, We're Pregnant. Now What?*

In the few days since we received our positive pregnancy test results, little has actually changed beyond the newly found inability to stop smiling. We have told only a couple people about our joyous news owing to the myriad things that can go wrong in the first trimester. Especially given how our luck has run to date, we want to be very cautious about telling anyone too early.

The morning we found out, Lucy was kind enough to tell me before her boss, whom she is close with, but I was first only by a gnat's ass. Since I was in the shower when the positive test results came back, there were a few precious minutes where the need to tell someone almost caused Lucy's head to actually split open. Her computer was booted up and her boss was available on instant-message, so it was a very close call. A single instant of clarity stopped Lucy from hitting the Enter key after she typed *I'm pregnant!* in the messaging window. In that moment, she decided her husband really should know first. I know what you're thinking and you're right: it was very magnanimous of her to wait.

So, once I knew, Lucy then instant-messaged her boss with the news. Her boss, as was customary, immediately called and started screaming at her. (Her boss is a woman, by the way. Women are morally and legally bound to scream at any woman who says she's pregnant. If they are face-to-face when the news breaks, they have to jump-hug too.) I told one of my team members—the one with the two kids I mentioned earlier—since she had been so helpful talking us through the earlier struggles. I sorta figured she'd paid her dues and deserved to hear the good news. Shortly afterward, I told another colleague of mine who also had given Lucy and me some wonderful advice and had acted as a sounding board.

Unbeknownst to me, I had broken some sort of good-news-equal-distribution rule by telling two people to Lucy's one, so she told me she got to tell someone else. The only person she could think of who was not going to be forced to tell anyone else was a colleague of hers. (As this colleague was a man, he did not have to scream at her.)

Once the universe was back in equilibrium, we were able to refocus—and start wondering just how many landmines there are that could cause us problems over the next couple months. I also began trying to figure out how to hermetically seal Lucy in a glass chamber to shield her from all germs, organisms, or other dangers without suffocating her. I figured, being a persistent guy, I could eventually get there.

I have started checking some of those Web sites that show us how to plan for a baby. One—babycenter.com—has a calculator that shows the current stage of development of your baby. Ours is still in zygote stage. I'm very proud.

# 16

## *It's Confirmed: We Have a Zygote*

Our first post-fertilization visit to the GYNie was this week. The doctor could not see us, as she had to go and do an emergency C-section (if I had a nickel for every time I've heard *that* one), so we saw the nurse practitioner instead. The nurse was a really pleasant woman who was very cheerful and helpful. We had plenty of questions, which she answered patiently and completely. Even my sarcastic ones! It was great.

The main purpose for this visit was to do our first ultrasound and confirm that Lucy really was pregnant and that all was right with the world. I'd always heard the quality of ultrasounds rumored to be incredibly poor, and I'd seen on TV and in movies where people look at them, eagerly searching and squinting for the thing that is their baby-to-be—never sure they actually see it but hoping they do. They were always shocked that the little speck they're looking at is actually something they're going to be cleaning up the feces of someday.

This was, of course, my first experience with one of these devices firsthand, so I wasn't entirely sure what to expect. As it turned out, we could actually see, fairly easily, what the nurse was looking at. In fact, it was obvious *what* was going to be turning into a baby in the not too distant future. What was less obvious was *how* it was going to turn into a baby. So far, it was not much more than a speck surrounded by a black oval.

Obviously, we couldn't see hair or eye color or anything, but I could see all of the necessary proof that Lucy was, in fact, knocked up. Our little zygote was two millimeters in length.

After getting our copy of the picture, we walked into the nurse's office, where she handed us a small rainforest's worth of reading material. Good thing we had thirty-five weeks to read through all of this because there was no less than twelve pounds of documentation and literature to get through. Who knew getting pregnant was going to leave us with so much homework?

Neither Lucy nor I had been saying it, but we were both pretty nervous about going in for this appointment. We'd had so many disappointments that we were just waiting for the other shoe to drop. Had the nurse said, "Hey, wait a minute, there's nothing here," neither of us would've been all that shocked. However, the devastation would've been noticed on the Richter scale. Imagine our relief then when she said, "Everything looks perfect for this stage." She did warn us that there's still plenty of time for things to go wrong, but at least she was kind enough to do it in that matter-of-fact and don't-you-worry-about-it sort of way.

On the drive home, Lucy was giddy. With real proof in hand that we were expecting—and reams of literature to boot—we felt we could actually talk about it in real terms, if only between ourselves. Lucy began trying to convince me we should tell her family during Thanksgiving next week, but I was dead-set against it. If possible, they were going to be even more excited than us.

Her family is Italian, you see, and this is going to be the first child in the next generation of their family. I just couldn't deal with breaking their hearts if anything should go wrong. I really hope Lucy can keep a lid on it. Granted, I don't think she can, but I've certainly been wrong before.

I can see it now as we walk up to her parents' or her aunt and uncle's house on Monday:

Me: "Okay now, really, we can't tell them. Okay? When they ask, just say, 'No news yet. When we have some, you'll be the first to know.' It's not a lie, okay?"

Lucy: "Okay, *jeez!* You've only told me this like a thousand times already!"

Them: "Hi! Oh, it's *so* good to see you!"

Lucy: "*We're pregnant!*"

Actually, I'm being too hard on Lucy here. The truth is, if she cracks, it won't be like that. More likely, they'll ask, and she'll just sit there grinning ear to ear and shaking eagerly like a high school cheerleader waiting for the rest of the squad to notice her brand-new hickey.

Oh well, I can hope.

# 17

# *Medical Degrees and Math Skills*

The nurse practitioner at the GYNie's office was very poor at math. Of this, I became convinced. Through keen powers of deduction and counting on our fingers, she, Lucy, and I decided the date of conception was October 22. Our conversation was happening on November 16. During this conversation she said, "Okay, that makes you between five and six weeks pregnant." I'm pretty sure she was on crack. I wasn't exactly the mathematician of the group, but when I counted the weeks, I got we were coming up on four weeks.

In fact, the morning we had the positive test result, I even counted ahead based on weeks (also using the October 22 conception date) and determined the due date would be July 29 (more or less). The nurse practitioner, however, using her funky Gyno-colorian calendar, put it at July 15. Note: we have our first book on pregnancy now, and it confirmed that a conception date of October 22 would give us a due date of July 29. Ha! *In your face* medical degree!

- Score
  - Bill = 1
  - Trained specialist = 0

---

Note from later:

Eventually, I found out the reason for the discrepancy was due to the point from which one starts counting weeks. While we started counting from the date of probable conception, the doctors count from the start of the woman's cycle. So, in effect, we're both right. I'm still taking the point though.

---

# 18

## *They're Right, But So What?*

Everyone out in the world who has successfully done something (anything) will be happy to foist upon someone else unsuccessfully trying to do the same thing some piece of advice, which, unsolicited though it may be, they are certain the receiver will be thrilled to receive. Now that we have successfully achieved conception, I will offer up my own little bit of unsolicited input for any of you who may have similar difficulties getting knocked up.

So many times while we were trying to conceive, people would toss at us the following completely unhelpful advice: "Try not to think about it, and try not to get stressed about it." Wow. Thanks for that. Obviously, this is completely useless advice, as there is no way to not think about something that is at the forefront of your mind, right? Sadly, I can now tell you, these folks may be absolutely right.

When dealing with all of this crap, I can now say one really needs a mind-set reset button. (Side note: if you're having trouble conceiving and you've been at it less than a year, and you don't have prior knowledge of an issue that will make getting pregnant difficult, definitely take a breather. You're probably not actually having trouble yet. A good doctor won't even see you for the purpose of trying to find a problem until you've been trying unsuccessfully for at least a year.) If you've been trying for longer than a year without success, do yourself a favor and figure out what really relaxes you or really gets your mind in another place, even for just a short time. A friend of mine would say, "Go on vacation." We didn't, but I suspect now that if we'd taken that approach, the conception process might have been shortened.

I have no idea why, but for some reason, over-thinking this process and stressing about it is absolutely the best way to ensure you won't be easily successful. I don't get how this interferes with biology, but it does. Now that I think about it, maybe this is why teenagers so often get in trouble. They're not trying, and they're not stressed about it.

Find some way to stop thinking about it as a job and you just may find yourself with child. Sadly, there's no way to *completely* stop thinking about it during this time, but do try. Maybe get really drunk.

# 19

## *Ah Yes, Morning Sickness*

In some ways, Lucy's bout thus far with morning sickness hasn't been nearly as bad as is so often described by others. There hasn't yet been any vomiting, but there has been this underlying theme of nausea and exhaustion to her days. It sucks for her, of course, because nausea is a part of her every waking moment now, and she can only get over it for short periods by eating some crackers. (The nurse practitioner gave Lucy some suckers that were supposed to help. She tried one, said it tasted like shit, and threw it out.) Since receiving the good news, I now hear no less than once every five minutes a heavy sigh followed by, "Man, I feel like shit!" Sometimes, just the sigh.

This is obviously a real bummer for Lucy, but hey, it sucks for me too! I just want to help out here—you know, be a part of it all and do what I can to make Lucy's journey a touch easier. Well, it turns out there is absolutely zero I can do. I do offer my obligatory, "Anything I can do, honey?" knowing full well there isn't. I feel pretty helpless here.

A bit of advice to the men here: when the mother of your zygote is vomiting due to morning sickness, at least feign concern. Give her a sorrowful look and a gentle pat on her knee. It's really all you've got to work with, so you might as well fire that shot across the bow.

I've decided the very best thing I can do is enjoy *my* meals just as much as I can and make certain Lucy knows how good my food is, seeing as she can't eat much herself right now. At least if she sees me happy, she, as my spouse, will feel better, right? Yes, I'm sure this is right.

# 20

## *Turkey Day Come and Gone*

We got back from a weeklong trip visiting her family this morning. Lucy
was a champ. With her promise firmly in place not to tell anyone, she
lasted a respectable two and a half hours at her aunt and uncle's house
before peppering me with, "Come on, let's tell them. Pleeeeeeease!
Come on, come on, come on ..." over and over again, accompanied by
the pouty lip. I held my ground though, even when she tried to turn
it back on me by saying, "You know, you're really upsetting me right
now."

Ironically, especially given how much we'd prepared for *the*
question, this turned out to be the first visit in over a year where not
one person asked if we were pregnant. It was almost scary. I was certain
that everyone, aware of our struggles to date, either individually or
collectively decided not to ask anymore. This was, of course, a great
help. If you'd have told me a week ago we'd leave a visit with her family
without anyone knowing, I'd have said you were certifiably nuts.
Suddenly, however, this was looking like a real possibility.

Eventually, Lucy did tell one person, who, for the sake of
maintaining family unity, shall remain nameless, but she stopped short
of telling anyone else. While visiting, I realized she needs someone to
talk with who's coming from a female perspective—someone who can
plan and commiserate with her—and I just don't fall into that category
on any level. I figured that I had been being a bit hard-lined on this
"don't tell anyone" plan, even if it's for everyone's sake. Maybe more
to the point, I also realized that it was only a matter of time before
Lucy stopped listening to me at all on this matter and started telling

folks. At least this way, it felt more like a capitulation instead of an unconditional surrender.

Of course, if members of either her family or mine find out that one person knew ahead of them, it could cause some genuine issues. If and when that happens, I hope they understand that the pain of having to disappoint the expectations of a family the size of Lucy's (should the worst happen) would be more than we can handle. I hope they can understand we are being tightlipped out of emotional need. However, I'm already planning on ordering a bunch of copies of this book with this section omitted just in case.

Getting through the holiday without everyone knowing—or at least, without them verbalizing a suspicion—was a true act of will for Lucy. Given the vast expanse of food her family serves for holidays, that ever present feeling of nausea meant she required incredible strength to eat "normally" so as not to rouse suspicion. She was also taking three-hour naps randomly, though fortunately, typically when others were busily occupied. All in all, I think it was a successful trip, as she found a female confidant and still managed to do a fine job protecting our sort-of secret.

I'm pretty excited for Christmas now. Getting to tell everyone in that here-is-some-awesome-news sort of way should be a blast and a real moment for Lucy that she's earned.

# 21

## *God Bless the Guy That Invented Saltines*

Lucy's bout of morning sickness was becoming less "morning" and more "sickness" with each passing day. The other night, I suddenly noticed she had quietly snuck out of the room while we were watching TV. When I found her, she was hunched over the toilet getting ready to puke. Once again, I was left feeling there was precious little I could do to ease her situation. I stood there for a short while then, finally, decided to help the only way I reasonably could: I held her hair back while she dry-heaved. (The scene was vaguely reminiscent of our wedding night, except that she was actually puking that night and I didn't have to really hold her hair thanks to all the hairpins she had in. It should be noted that, on that night, her condition was consumption-related and had nothing to do with any status changes in her life that had occurred that day. Of course, I can't promise the overconsumption was entirely unrelated to her recent status changes, but there you are.)

Eventually I found a way to contribute, if only a small amount. I went downstairs to grab some saltine crackers for her. Here's another small piece of advice: the moment you find out your lady is with child, do everyone a favor and stock up on crackers. These things are lifesavers. Whenever you find yourself in a restaurant that gives the little packages with their soup, pocket as many as you can without being noticed or crushing the crackers. These little packages are very handy to have around in a pinch. I have taken to keeping them in my glove box, my computer bag, my coat pockets, etc.

The challenge for Lucy going forward is that she is so queasy most of the time that she has no appetite or inclination to eat anything. In a bout of nature-irony, this lack of food ratchets her queasy feeling up to actual nausea. She does the right thing and tries to eat something when she can to settle her stomach, but it's definitely a challenge for her. If it weren't for crackers and antacids, she might not eat for the full forty weeks.

# 22

## *You Know What I Meant*

Our pregnant friends in Germany called the other day. If I haven't mentioned it before, these are really great people and we're lucky to be able to call them friends. The wife, Chrissi, is slightly better or at least more comfortable with English than her husband, Carsten, who is still considerably better with English than either of us are with German. (All the German I know comes from episodes of *Hogan's Heroes* and Tool songs. *Und keine eier!*)

They are expecting a baby themselves right now and have been offering their support during our struggles, so we went ahead and let them in on our secret a while ago. Plus, seeing as they're in Germany, they can't tell anyone here at home.

Despite her near mastery of English, Chrissi still has the occasional difficulty with subtle meanings that are so important. Example: when she called us the other day, she started the conversation off with, "Hello. I just wanted to make sure your baby was still alive."

Naturally, we got her intended meaning, but it did give us both a chuckle (which caused Lucy to have to throw up). It was a very entertaining and nice moment.

# 23

## *No No, Seriously, That's Your Baby's Heart!*

The week after Thanksgiving was supposed to be the week we got to see the baby's heartbeat for the first time. This would've put us right in at week six, where the heart first resembles a little blinky LED light. (As proof that I'm reading the material we obtained, let me share an interesting fact: I've come to learn the heart is not four-chambered at this stage as it will be soon, a detail that will become critical later if we are to give birth to a human.) Unfortunately, I was called away for a short business trip to Korea, so we had to wait another week to make this visit to the GYNie.

Earlier I mentioned that Lucy and I have been very nervous each step of this journey so far. At no point would either of us be surprised to find out there's a problem—devastated, of course, but not altogether surprised. The extra week, therefore, was something of a frustration for both of us.

As before, the appointment at the GYNie went well and without incident. Our baby-in-progress had changed from a speck to a jellybean. We could see the heart flickering quite quickly—just a tiny LED blinking away. The GYNie kindly supplemented the description of what she saw on the screen with plenty of descriptives like, "perfect," and, "excellent," and, "this is exactly what we should be seeing." She's a peach, that GYNie.

Later that day, I was talking with the colleague of mine who knows of our pending family addition. She told me she'd been secretly very worried about this trip to the GYNie ever since I told her we didn't see the heart beating in the first ultrasound. Wisely, she chose not to mention this concern. The only material we have on this very clearly states that the earliest one can hope to see the heart beating is week six, so we weren't too concerned given that our first ultrasound was on the first day of week five.

# 24

## *Congratulations, You Have a Gummi Bear.*

Owing to the fact that nothing really notable transpired in the past three weeks, I skipped ahead in this journal to a few days before Christmas. At a check-in with the GYNie, Lucy and I decided to do one more ultrasound before going to visit her family for the holiday. This one was not really necessary, but we just wanted to have a more substantial picture to show everyone when we finally told them the news.

Especially in comparison to the last ultrasound, this one was amazing. Where the last one was a jellybean-shaped mass with a flickering spot in the middle, this was a distinctive baby in the making. Head, body, arms, and legs were all easily identifiable. It was really amazing to see something that looked like it would actually end up being our baby some day.

Our former jellybean was still very rounded though. Arms and legs were plump little balls on the side of a larger plump little ball, which had a still larger ball for a head. The GYNie explained that we're in the, "Gummi bear stage of appearance." Sure enough, it looked exactly like a Gummi bear minus the snout and pointed ears. (Good thing for that, in my opinion.)

When I compared the three ultrasounds, I really gained an appreciation for how much was happening in these ovens and how quickly. The first picture of our baby-to-be really showed a black oval surrounding a white speck. The second showed something like a small jellybean (probably vanilla, maybe coconut). In the third, we had a human Gummi bear. Incredible. All of this change in just a shade under five weeks blew me away.

Lucy's overall health has remained more or less unchanged. Generally speaking, she's just not feeling well. She can't eat red meat at all right now—or even think about eating it—and she feels like puking most of the time. Up from the previous five minutes, now every four minutes on the dot, she emits a heavy sigh followed by, "Man, I feel like shit."

Also, everything smells around one hundred times stronger to her than any nonpregnant person. I figure this makes her sense of smell about as strong as that of a Springer Spaniel. This means she wouldn't make a good drug-sniffing assistant for the DEA but is handy to have around when checking if milk is bad without even having to open the fridge. Everything smells. *Everything.* Either good or bad but certainly everything smells. Our dog, a black Lab named Ripley, apparently smells worse than any other living animal, but I, being a mere nonpregnant mortal, have senses far too dull to be aware of it myself. I, it would seem, am the lucky one. (I have no idea why Ripley is unaware of how bad she smells given her olfactory senses are still greater than Lucy's.)

Fortunately, just as the GYNie predicted, Lucy's needing less sleep. Where, immediately after realizing she was pregnant, she was sleeping on average about sixteen hours a day, she's back to something more normal now. She's also getting her energy back, which is good, as she has a lot of things that smell terrible to document.

As you can imagine, I've had very few true responsibilities of late beyond trying to find new and creative places to put saltines so that they can be had at a moment's notice but not get crushed. (Latest: sunglass compartment in her car.) Sure, I try to look concerned and empathetic when she's really sick, but that's less a responsibility than a survival mechanism.

# 25

## *An Ominous Sign*

The other night, Lucy was in the bedroom sleeping when I got home from work. I was watching TV and talking with my sister-in-law, who was visiting, when I received the following text message from Lucy, *Can you bring me a piece of cheese, please?*

I realized she was tired and sick and all those other first trimester pregnancy-related things so I was trying to be mindful and help where I could, but *seriously!* Did she really just text me from the next room to bring her cheese?

When I went into the bedroom to give her grief about texting me with something like that, she was laughing. Then she gave me the pouty, "Aw, come on … I'm sick and I'm tired, and your baby wants cheese!"

This is a bad sign.

# 26

## *The Everything Sucks Stage*

We traveled to Denver to visit Lucy's family for the Christmas holiday. Telling everyone was a blast; it was exactly what Lucy needed. There were plenty of tears, screams, and hugs. The men all handed me beers (not simultaneously) and congratulated me with a hearty clink of the bottle. All conversations for the remainder of the week's visit were dutifully pregnancy-focused.

Denver has an interesting effect on my wife, though. She's from Denver originally but truly hates it there. She hates the weather, she hates the look of it, and she hates the word "Denver" and any word that rhymes with it. The only thing Denver has going for it is Lucy's family. Every time we go for a visit, Lucy's torn between wanting to move close to her family and never wanting to step foot on Denver soil again. The longer the gap between visits, the more Lucy misses her family and wants to be around them. Every time we get there, though, within twelve minutes of leaving the Denver airport, she's mumbling exasperatedly about how much she hates it there.

This trip, however, both of these conditions were exaggerated by Lucy's increased hormonal state and general condition of not feeling well, resulting in more dramatic longing for family surroundings preflight and louder complaints about all things Denver post-arrival. I know what you're thinking: "What fun for Bill!" Well, you'd be spot on.

At one point late in the week, while driving down I-25, Lucy launched into a seven-minute-long uninterrupted diatribe of the many things that were, at that moment, freaking her out, pissing her off, or just depressing her. Seven minutes. I timed it, unbeknownst to her.

Everything was there, from the blizzard we were driving in, to our dog having diabetes, to what we may or may not be able to afford once the baby arrives. There was absolutely nothing I could add to the conversation that didn't result in a new painful and twisted turn.

I realized my mistake at one point and quickly took a new approach. You see, there was no way to make Lucy feel good, any more than there was a way to make the blizzard stop. That wasn't the point of the conversation. She was venting—venting about what exactly, she didn't know, but there was surely no way to cap it until the venting had ceased of its own accord. From that moment on, the conversation took a rather pleasant turn, at least for me. Inwardly I focused all of my attention on timing how long Lucy could continue without my saying anything and on keeping our rental car from spinning out of control (for a second time that trip), but outwardly I kept a mask of interest on my face. My looking concerned kept her from killing me in a hormone-induced rage, so she vented and I survived. It was a win/win.

The trip to Denver was interesting for one other reason. It was during this trip, a mere ten to eleven weeks into the pregnancy, I realized I was already starting to think fatherly thoughts. During a blizzard one evening, we were traveling up I-25 at a decent clip of thirty-five miles per hour. We were in the left lane traveling on a nearly straight stretch when we suddenly, without my touching the brakes or gas or even moving the wheel, began spinning clockwise. We spun what felt like ten times (I wasn't counting), traveling all the way from the left lane to the far right lane then back to the far left lane and coming to a stop on the left shoulder facing the correct direction. The sheer physics of the event were mind-boggling considering we didn't hit any cars, snow bank, signs, or anything else that would have made me instantly regret not getting the rental insurance.

From the moment I realized I was no longer in control of the car, my mind immediately jumped to the fact that Lucy was in the back seat. All that went through my mind, over and over again until the car came to a stop was, "Holy crap! My wife and baby are in the back seat, I can't let anything happen to them!" It was a very surreal moment in retrospect. I suddenly felt as though I were a father or at least thinking like one. (Well, I felt that way once I could let go of the steering wheel.)

# Part Three

## The Second Trimester: The Eye of the Storm

# 27

## *Holy Crap, It's a BABY!*

A couple days after returning from the Christmas trip to Denver, New Years Day was upon us. The next day, January 2, was significant for two reasons:

1. It was Lucy's birthday.

2. It was the first day of the second trimester.

With these milestones upon us, we were ready for changes. First, we'd been told that once a pregnancy got to this stage, the chances of encountering significant problems dropped to around 5 percent. Second, Lucy's GYNie told us that Lucy would likely start to feel a lot better. She explained this was when the overwhelming tiredness would start to ebb and the morning sickness would also start to let up. Sure enough, the day after her birthday, when we were scheduled to see the doctor for an NT (Nuchal Translucency) Test, Lucy called me at the office prior to the appointment and said she felt, "really good!" She had some of her appetite back and was, for the first time in five or six weeks, not feeling like she would fall asleep the instant she sat down.

We also got a second dog at this time. Our Lab, Ripley, was going to be nine when the baby arrives, and, not wanting her to be suddenly hurting for attention, we decided to get her a playmate. So we've adopted Samantha (we didn't name her). All in all, lots of changes in the house right now.

Back to the doctor's visit. The purpose of this visit was to perform a higher-resolution ultrasound, the aforementioned NT scan, to check for the likelihood of Down syndrome. This was done by measuring the gap between the baby's spine and outside of the neck. The NT scan measurements, which one received immediately, would be combined with blood test results, which wouldn't be available for around two weeks. While the NT scan alone gave the doctor some indication of the likelihood of Down syndrome, it's the combination of the two tests that gave an overall risk assessment. We had our own purpose here, however: checking out our baby. There was at least a chance we'd be able to tell if it was a boy or girl, so added bonus!

The scan was simply the most amazing thing I'd ever seen. What had once been a speck, then a jelly bean, then a Gummi bear, was now an actual, no-kidding baby-in-the-making. Easily identifiable head, arms, legs, hands, and feet were all present and accounted for. Our baby's spine was so identifiable in all of its complex wonder that we were stunned. The baby was also moving quite a bit and the heart was flickering away. I was overcome with the significance of what I was seeing—truly speechless. I'd often seen movies that depict viewing the ultrasound images as a very emotional moment for people, but I never really understood it until then.

For you, there are some important things to keep in mind when going in for this NT test: most notable is that, it doesn't tell you one way or another if your child is going to be born with Down syndrome—it's only a risk assessment. A positive result on this test shows a woman has a higher likelihood of giving birth to a baby with Down syndrome, but it does *not* say that she absolutely will.

My point is, be careful how much sleep you lose over the results. I'm not saying don't take the test; just don't work yourself up too much in advance. From all the research I have found so far, the odds of a woman at thirty-three (Lucy's age when our baby arrives) having a baby with Down syndrome are around 1 in 570. So if the scan comes back showing a strong likelihood, it's really just increasing already low odds, though you still get to suffer through the next two weeks waiting for the blood test results. Had I known all this before the test, I don't think I would have been so nervous going into it.

One of my colleagues later told me her son's NT measurement had come back showing a high likelihood for Down syndrome. The doctor performing the scan was very concerned and she, understandably, freaked out. The blood test later showed her baby's chances of being born with Down syndrome were very low, however. The previous indicator was just an anomaly in the NT scan. (Her baby did not have Down syndrome, by the way.)

Remember, even with the two tests combined though, it's still a risk assessment, not a diagnosis. If they come back showing a concern, you can do more tests to be certain, but these are more invasive, and possibly somewhat dangerous. And really, what's the benefit of knowing this, I say. It's not like you can fix the issue once you know. So you wait, worry, and suffer to no purpose.

Of course, after all this explanation of why you shouldn't worry, I have to admit we were still very relieved when our scan was perfect. In fact, the doctor said the view was so good, he'd even have been able to tell if the baby was going to be born with spina bifida (which also was a happy negative). Given how worked up we were going into the appointment, though, I'm sure a positive indication for risk would've sent us over the edge. And again I say, what would the point have been? There would have been nothing we could've done at that moment but worry. After the appointment, we decided, if the blood tests also came back with no concerning indicators, we wouldn't do any more optional tests. (Note from later: Two weeks later, the blood tests came back fine.)

We did ask the doctor if he could tell the gender. He couldn't tell for sure because our baby was essentially lying on its stomach, legs pulled in and arms tucked up. Bummer. He did say that, if he had to hazard a guess, he'd guess it was a girl. But that's purely a guess.

His guess might not sound like much to go on, but to be honest, at no time since learning Lucy was pregnant have I considered, even for a moment, that we might have a boy. Part of this is just an odd feeling on the matter, and part of it is due to family history: my generation in my family appears genetically incapable of producing boys. Time will tell whether I'm right, but I'm just feeling a girl's on the way.

While on the topic of gender, I find it strange and humorous that every tiny detail of my wife's pregnancy is interpreted by someone as an indication of the gender of our unborn baby. A few of the things I've heard so far:

- "Oh, Lucy's sick all the time but not actually vomiting? That means it's a girl."

- "She's tired all the time? Oh yeah, it's a boy."
- "The baby's legs were crossed during the ultrasound? Yep, it's a girl."
- "Lucy got pulled over on the 101 for going 78 in a 65? *Definitely* a boy."

I suppose one of the things I find funniest is that this input is never solicited. I can't imagine anyone walking up to a random co-worker and saying, "Hey, Ted, you seem like a bright fellow, question for you: my wife, who's four months pregnant, is really gassy all the time, plus, at the latest ultrasound, the baby was facing to the side rather than the front. Does this give you any indication as to the gender of our baby?"

I wish I knew why people did this. It's a bit silly.

# 28

## *A Painful Note Unrelated to Pregnancy*

Note: If you are not a "dog person" or a "pet person" of some sort and don't understand why people become emotionally attached to their pets, please feel free to skip to the next section.

Because we don't have enough going on to emotionally tax us at the moment, five days after the amazing NT ultrasound appointment, our beautiful black Lab, Ripley, died of a sudden and very violent sickness. She was only eight, and, apart from having diabetes and being overweight—as Labs tend to be—she was in perfect health.

Ripley was our girl—our family. We'd had her since she was seven weeks old, and she was 100 percent ours. She had so much personality; she seemed to understand what we meant and what we wanted beyond what we could put into words. She refused to allow either Lucy or me to be in a bad mood and just wanted to be around us and be happy. She was the dog that everyone loved to be around. Even those occasional visitors who were deathly afraid of dogs prior to meeting her would soon be seen absentmindedly patting her head. Rip seemed to take it as a personal challenge to get them over their fears.

We love her and miss her terribly. Not having her here with us has truly broken our hearts, and I am sad beyond my previous understanding of the word. I had so wanted her to be our young daughter's canine guardian and friend, and now those family plans are out the window unexpectedly.

Oftentimes, when one loses a pet, one can say, "They were old and had a great life" or "They were really sick; they're not hurting any more." Well, Rip hadn't been suffering from any long, protracted illness or hurting, though I do like to think she had a great life. She was in her prime and loved to wrestle and play and carry her leash herself when on a walk. She frolicked. She enjoyed everything. There is nothing we can take from this that makes it better in any way, and I'm left with only bitterness about it.

Okay, I'm done now.

# 29

## *One More Try, and Now We Wait*

Another trip to the GYNie for a monthly checkup is upon us. These have turned out to be very valuable in that they get me out of the office for an extended lunch even though the visits tend to last no more than twenty minutes. Perfect. Plus, my favorite restaurant in the known universe is on the way back from the doctor's office, so that's where we usually eat lunch on these days. Perfect again.

Once again, the visit goes without incident. A bullet point summary would be:

- Sign in
- Lucy pees in a cup (I do not)
- Lucy stands on a scale to weigh in (I make a stupid boxing/weigh-in joke)
- Lucy and I go into a room, where a nurse takes Lucy's blood pressure (she does not take mine)
- We wait five minutes for the GYNie to come in (I make insipid and probably not funny sarcastic comments)
- Doc comes in, looks over many pieces of paper, makes a comment about Lucy not yet gaining any weight but says everything looks great
- We ask some forced questions
- Doc listens to baby's heartbeat
- Doc tells us to go to a lab to do one test or another
- We leave

Total time is around twenty minutes from ding to dong.

Ever notice how when you get your blood pressure taken the nurse feels the need to tell you what it is? "Hmmm, you're at 150 over 88." What the hell am I supposed to do with this information? Should I be taking notes? Doesn't the nurse write this stuff down somewhere? Am I supposed to be chronicling all of this from day one?

I'm afraid one day the GYNie will ask me, "Bill, quick, what was Lucy's blood pressure on January 18?" When I don't have it noted in a flipbook of some variety, which is filled with notes on various and sundry details from daily blood pressure to time and volume of every time Lucy has urinated since conception, I will be chastised unmercifully and proclaimed an unfit father and my child's life will be ruined before it's even seen the world outside the womb.

I'm convinced the nurse tells you this information for no other purpose but to lord it over you that she knows something you do not.

Eventually, the doc comes in and goes about the ceremony of making sure we're good to go—we are— and we again ask if she wouldn't mind giving us an ultrasound, however unnecessary it may be, to see if she can tell the sex of the baby. She obliges but says she still can not tell. We're disappointed but not altogether surprised. I suppose we'll wait for the twenty-week ultrasound. This is annoying though because that's still five weeks away and this information is very important. I don't know why, but it really, really is. Lucy's entire family is, I'm sure, sitting by their computers, credit cards in hand, just waiting to send us little gifts, and all they need to know is pink or blue. This is critical stuff, kid. Can't you just open up the legs for a second and give us a look real quick? (Wow, that sounds way too pedophile-esque for my own comfort. This is a question I hope my kid never actually hears from anyone.)

# 30

# *The* Knocked Up *Incident*

Rather than going out to a movie last night, as was the plan, Lucy and I decided to stay in and watch a movie here at home. We added some new ones to our collection this past Christmas, so it was time to open one of them up. We opted for comedy and eventually decided on *Knocked Up*. We'd seen it before, sure, but both of us could watch a good movie more than once, and we remembered it being really enjoyable, so it was on. Bad decision.

Guys out there, another piece of advice: if your significant other is pregnant with your first child, you *must not* watch this movie during her pregnancy. Don't do it. Hide the movie somewhere until after the baby is on the outside. Any other forty weeks of your lives this movie is funny and entertaining, but *not* when you're expecting your first child.

You see, Lucy has been more than a touch anxious about the rapid changes that will be inflicted upon her person over these forty weeks. The added weight, stretch marks, and various things along those lines are really freaking her out. It doesn't help that my wife is a petite 5'2" and is carrying the offspring of a 6'3" guy. To date, she's been handling this pretty well, but the movie, which does such a great job of depicting how much the female goes through, suddenly freaks Lucy out clean and proper.

Of course, I made a *huge* mistake watching it with her, which didn't help a bit. Late in the movie, when Katherine Heigl's character is right around popping time, she's wearing a tank-top and turns sideways. It was then that I noticed she was, conservatively, only one-fifth smaller in circumference than she was in height. In spite of my keen understanding of how huge a mistake this was, I said aloud, "My *God!*" Big mistake. Huge. It was out of my mouth before I could stop it.

Then, during the delivery scene, the actress did such an excellent job of screaming holy terror that by the end of it Lucy was sobbing uncontrollably and telling me how scared she was. I was stuck. What was I supposed to do here? This was a train that'd left the station. I couldn't exactly say, "Well, maybe we'll look into a surrogate." I was a bit worried here that I would find no words of wisdom to help calm her. Fortunately, before I ruined everything trying, I came to a realization similar to the one I had in Denver: there were no perfect words of wisdom, so I needed to keep quiet for the most part. As soon as I understood that nothing I could say would help beyond, "No matter what, honey, I'll be right there with you" (still hoping that, in some language "right there with you" can be translated to "at a Rush concert"), it took a lot of the pressure off. It also prevented me from saying anything stupid and turning it into a "what the hell did I do?" discussion. I waited a bit until she was much calmer and then made some sarcastic comment to break the tension. It's helpful to have a reputation for being a somewhat insensitive jerk that spews sarcasm 90 percent of the time.

Oh, by the way, there were two scenes in that movie that really jarred me as well. The first was when the two heroes of the movie were sitting in their GYNie's office for an appointment, and the room was full of pregnant ladies looking miserable and parents with infants. There was this one baby that I swear wasn't done yet. Honestly, I think they took it out too soon. This had to be the strangest looking baby ever to grace the silver screen. I'm sure the child is perfectly beautiful now and will be a super model or rocket scientist or something else equally awe-inspiring, but as an infant, it was shockingly odd looking. I will probably be stunned into silence if our baby looks like that; I will be flummoxed beyond the ability to communicate. (Though, I wonder if the baby equivalent of beer goggles will cause me to believe my baby is absolutely beautiful no matter what. You know how all parents do that.). If you haven't seen the movie, and your woman isn't pregnant, check it out for this alone.

The other jarring moment for me was during the delivery scene. Cruelly, the director went out of his way to do a spectacular job of showing the delivery in gory detail. The word "crowning" was most definitely a correct description. I'm sure it was fake. Of course it was fake, but it was really, really well done.

You will recall from earlier that I'm a squeamish person. Seeing a baby crown, even a well done obvious fake, is very disturbing to me. Of course, I'm 100 percent certain the director put this in the movie for the sole purpose of causing an entire theater audience to simultaneously gag and cover their eyes. How am I so sure this was his purpose? Well, they just cut to it quickly—no panning and no warning—once and then cut to it again. Then they cut to it a third time! There can be no other reason for doing this except that they hoped to get a puker in the audience. When we saw it in the theater, I nearly jumped out of my seat at the first image. At least when we saw it this time, I was prepared and kept my eyes shut. I'm hoping Lucy didn't notice this, as it would probably not help her nervousness about the entire pending event.

# 31

## *It's a Girl! Well, Maybe.*

We had another monthly checkup this week. All in all, it went well. All of Lucy's various indicators were indicating no problems, and there was nothing to raise an eyebrow about. Lucy was also definitely starting to show by that point, which was exciting for us both. More than the ultrasounds, it made it all real in a very tangible way.

Various blood tests all came back normal, and the urine tests were not yet showing any signs of sugar level problems. (According to the book I've been consulting on a regular basis, the first signs of sugar level problems, also known as gestational diabetes, don't typically show until the third trimester, so I wasn't worried.) The only concern, if one could even call it that, was that Lucy was not gaining enough weight yet. In fact, she had not gained a pound since the date of conception. Lucy was instructed to try and eat smaller snacks more often throughout the day. Healthy things like nuts and stuff. Seemed like a doctor's order that shouldn't have been too tough to keep. I began thinking a nice cinnamon roll might be in order from time to time.

During the visit, we once again asked the GYNie if she could fire up the ultrasound machine and see if she could determine the sex of the baby. She happily agreed. At this time, we're coming in at eighteen weeks. It's a touch early to tell, especially as the ultrasound machine in this doctor's office is not the Cadillac type that we got to use for the NT test, but we wanted to give it a shot.

Upon smearing the goop on Lucy's belly and firing up the machine (this doctor keeps the goop warmed, by the way, a nice touch), the doctor could see many of the expected things right away. Head, heart, arms, legs, spine, and so on were still all present and accounted for. The baby was also moving around a bit, which was great to see. Unfortunately for our immediate goal, the baby was basically facing Lucy's spine. Given that this was the same problem we had at the NT scan, I was beginning to think the little tyke was already trying to piss us off. At this rate, the baby was going to be in time-out the *moment* it was born!

The doc did look for a long while and, like the last one, said, "If I had to make a guess, I'd say it's a girl. I just don't see anything down here between the legs." As before, I take this as something of a confirmation of my earlier suspicions. This means, of course, precisely nothing.

So we settled in to wait the two weeks until we could do the twenty-week scan at the office with the Cadillac. Neat.

By the way, while in the office on this visit, I decided Lucy's GYNie is *awesome!* The reader may recall my issue with Lucy's plan to have a water birth. We've never discussed it with her GYNie, but as I said before, I've been secretly hoping doing so would prompt the doc to try and talk Lucy out of it. Turns out, trying was not necessary.

Sitting in her office after this unhelpful ultrasound, I brought it up. Lucy and I bantered about it for a moment, which made the doc looked up from her mountain of paperwork and ask, "What are you guys talking about?" I suggested Lucy tell her what she wanted to do, which she did. The doc quickly and dismissively said, "Oh, we don't do those at this hospital," then went about perusing her papers she had just looked up from. Lucy sat in stunned silence. Internally, I was doing a happy dance. Problem solved.

I realize I'm being insensitive here and that Lucy really wanted to do this. However, I also am completely certain that on the big day, Lucy would get into the tub of water and would immediately say, "Get me the *hell* out of here!" So I really think I'm saving us time, trouble, and money here. Another win/win.

- Score:
  - Bill = 2
  - Lucy = 1,332,546

# 32

## *Now We Know, It's a ...*

Oh come on, I couldn't just give it to you right in the chapter name, could I?

The twenty-week ultrasound came around and it was incredible. Possibly the most impressive aspect for this reporter actually happened right before the ultrasound began. With Lucy lying back on the examination table, shirt hiked up to allow for the pending ultrasound, I had my hands on her belly hoping to feel the baby move for the first time. Sure enough, just a moment's delay and I felt a very distinct kick. It was really something. It was an odd sort of feeling, to be sure (doubly so for Lucy I would think, although she's felt the baby move already a couple times). I can only say this added to the realness of the whole thing in a most amazing way.

During the ultrasound, our baby was moving around nearly constantly—moving its arms and legs, turning its head, opening and closing its mouth. It was incredible. At one point, we could see the baby opening and closing its hands repeatedly and then sticking its thumb in its mouth.

As with the NT scan, the medical purpose of this ultrasound was to ensure there were no developmental issues. This helped our agenda too because it meant the doctor spent no less than thirty minutes, instead of the usual few, moving the sensor around and around, getting as many angles as it took to see all he needed to see.

For me, one of the most awe-inspiring parts of the test was probably one of the simplest moments. He moved the sensor to see the baby's feet. At one point, the sensor had a view of the bottom of the baby's right foot all by itself. The baby was wiggling its toes continuously. I don't know why this struck me as so significant, but it made the entire thing much more personal and genuine.

One of the freakiest moments, ironically, was when the doctor brought the sensor over to view the baby's face from the front. Note that from the profile the baby's face in the ultrasound looked, well, pretty normal. The view was not unlike an x-ray but a little more abstract. The harder, denser, materials showed up most clearly, and the soft tissue was viewable but in that foggy outline sort of way as with x-rays. Therefore, the profile showed the jaw and nose, and the baby could be seen opening and closing its mouth. When we looked closer, we could see, in the foggy outline, the button nose that all babies have. We could see the mouth and cheeks. It was amazing. Simply amazing. However, from the front, the image was startlingly different. At this point in the baby's development, much of the bone material was not yet calcified and dense, the way we typically think of bone. This means the ultrasound didn't "see" it well. One would think the front view of the face would be a skull view. Not so. Much of the face was sort of a ghost-like image—a foggy, black-and-white hybrid of bone and tissue with two hollow looking areas where the eyes were. (Eyes, of course, didn't show up.) The appearance was somewhat jarring. Truthfully, it looked like a movie poster for a horror film.

The doctor gave us about twenty still shots from the ultrasound. Lucy and I agreed the ones of the baby's profile were our favorites and least likely to cause nightmares. We got some unusually good pictures, though. Right as the doctor was about to stop the test, the baby took both hands, clasped them together along the side of the face, and sort of held them there in a glamour-shot photo sort of way. The doctor stopped in midsentence when he saw our baby do this and said, "Oh wow, that's just too cute." He took a picture of it. Then, a moment later, the baby took its now clasped hands and rested them under its left cheek, as though resting. Again, the doctor said, "Wow, this is just weird. That's just the cutest thing I've ever seen."

Yep, that's my kid.

We were also provided a DVD recording of the ultrasound session, which we've already watched two additional times.

I've told several people now of our intention to find out the baby's gender in advance. The responses are pretty evenly divided into two obvious camps: those who agree it's a good idea and those who do not. As for me, I don't care what anyone else does. In my opinion, if someone wants to wait until the delivery to find out, hey, knock yourself out. Who am I to tell you differently? Want to be surprised? Then be surprised. Why, however, do the folks in that camp feel the need to tell me they think it's a bad idea to find out in advance? It's not like I'm running around outside a movie theater in the late seventies yelling, "Darth Vader is Luke's father!" spoiling it for everyone standing in line. (Apologies if anyone reading this still hasn't seen those movies.) Why do they feel I'm spoiling some mystical nature-surprise or ruining the bonding by doing so? I don't get this. Not that I feel the need to explain myself, but it's still a surprise, right? What's the difference between it being a surprise now or in the delivery room? Either way, we get that misty moment about it, and this way Lucy gets her misty moment when she's not in a drug-and-pain-induced stupor. Plus, this way we get to plan better.

Oh yeah, I almost forgot, it's a girl. (Big surprise.)

# 33

## *Can Someone Please Show Me How to Work This Stupid Thing?*

Armed with the knowledge that our baby is a girl, we set out to begin the process of compiling a list of the sundry crap we'll need when she arrives. To this end, we went to a baby store in our area that is commonly thought to be "the one" to go to. All I can say of this place is it's quite possibly the third-level of hell.

I will volunteer here that I am not a fan of crowds. In fact, when in large crowds, I feel my tension rising as surely as if it were a volume knob on a stereo someone is steadily turning up. I truly believe the average IQ of a crowd of people goes down as the number of people increases. It's definitely a total-less-than-the-sum-of-its-parts sort of thing. If the average IQ of thirty-five people is around 120 when they're alone, as soon as they come together, the group average somehow drops to 80. I'm sure there's some scientific explanation for this, but I am unaware of it. This is the case even here in the Bay Area, where if you're not a graduate of Stanford, MIT, or Berkeley, you're pariah and people won't be seen speaking to you in public for fear of being ostracized themselves. Once in a crowd, people lose the ability to navigate from point A to point B without bumping into me or suddenly stopping right in front of me, causing me to bump into them. All concepts of personal space go out the window in large crowds. As I said, my tension level rises, and, as it does, I get louder. I'm not proud but I'll admit it: I can be kind of a jerk in a situation like this, and Lucy wisely chooses to usher me out before I say something likely to get my ass kicked or thrown in jail.

Well, in a baby preparation store, I was quickly finding this set of circumstances increased tenfold. Again, I couldn't say why this was, but it seemed people just didn't care about anyone else while there and were, without remorse, walking right over another person to get to that baby stroller they'd been eyeing. I was quickly losing my patience. The problem was compounded by the fact that none of the people milling about and being generally problematic actually worked at the store. At one point, I was looking for someone to help me with a particularly complex looking stroller that, I'm a bit embarrassed to say, I couldn't figure out how to collapse to save my life. Unfortunately, I couldn't have found someone to help me if I'd left a trail of twenty-dollar bills for them to find me by.

A friend of mine, who had a son a little over a year ago, swore by this one model of stroller, so we decided to check it out. Upon finding it at one of the only stores in the entire Bay Area that carries it, we realized it could not be operated without an advanced engineering degree. We weren't alone on this, by the way; within a few minutes of my standing alongside the stroller of doom, there were no fewer than seven couples surveying it suspiciously. Each man had a go at figuring out how to collapse the thing or attach a different appendage. Not one of us could do it. By the way, this was a $900 stroller we were looking at. Maybe I was being a simpleton, but if I sold strollers and I suddenly had a crowd of people standing around the Rolls Royce of strollers, all failing to operate it correctly, I might—just maybe—have stepped in and given an impromptu demo. Certainly, if it was a choice between tearing myself away from sudoku for ten minutes to demo the thing or watching eight couples get pissed and walk out—as Lucy and I did—I might have found a way to make the demo happen. It seems the folks in this store did not share my business prowess.

I don't think this apathy toward potentially paying customers is localized to this store. I think it is a condition of living in the San Francisco Bay Area. See, there are so many people living here that no retail business actually needs any single customer. They figure, so what if this one guy—we'll call him Bill—gets pissed and walks out. No problem. There's a long line of people right behind Bill who are desperate to toss their money at the cash register like rice at a wedding and will likely be a lot less annoying and pissy about it than Bill (who, granted, wouldn't have been annoying and pissy if we'd simply acknowledged his existence, but hey, we're focusing on the problem now, not the cause). This way of thinking permeates all aspects of retail life here. I was in a restaurant once where, after receiving such bad service I felt I needed to mention it to management, the manager refused to talk with me. I said—very calmly and professionally, mind you—that I wanted to express a concern about the service I'd received, and the manager literally walked away from me without saying a word. This is a strange place, the Bay Area. It's a good place to visit, but I wouldn't want to live here.

We have been to three stores now trying to get a demo of this and other comparable strollers. In not one could we secure the coveted demo. As far as I'm concerned now, we're going to use a damn shopping cart. I'm not cruel, I'll throw a pillow and probably a blanket or two in the bottom, but I will not play this *Oh please, sir, may I give you some money for your table scraps* game the average consumer is forced to play here in the Bay. (Sadly, you and I both know the truth: at some point, I'll break down and find a way to get a demo of the things and will pick on one. I'll be doing it under protest though. Which means precisely jack.)

One further note: just as with everything else you do related to your coming baby, everyone will tell you which stroller, car seat, high chair, baby bottle, and diaper you "just have to use." To make things more confusing, everyone who takes it upon themselves to give this unrequested advice is very passionate about their choice. These folks are definitely brand loyal. Of course, if everyone has "the" one to get, and not one of the ones they say is "the" one is the same as what the next guy recommends, how do I know which is really "the" one? I'm going back to my earlier comments about listening to advice from various folks. Take advice from a few people you trust and start there. This has added a lot of homework for Lucy and me, though, as my plan of attack would have been to go to a store and buy the first thing that had four wheels and a place to put a baby (seeing as we'd never get a sales person to help us anyway).

One bit of advice on the stroller topic was particularly interesting though. Yesterday I talked with a friend of mine who I feel is—and I mean this—absolutely the smartest man I know. Ever met one of those people who seem to know something about a lot of things? Well, this person seems to know nearly everything about everything. I've never stumped him. His advice on strollers was, interestingly, not to get one at all. He said we'll spend most of our time with the baby strapped to our chest or back in a carrier or sling and carrying a diaper bag, and this approach is far superior to lugging a cumbersome stroller around. I like this advice: cheap, straightforward, and not brand loyal. This is a plan I'm going to have to look into.

# 34

## *Revisiting The "My Kids Won't Act This Way" Topic*

You may have noticed that I can be something of an opinionated jerk about some things. While this tendency may have slipped in from time to time, I've tried to not jump up on too many soap boxes, as I suspect you didn't start reading this book to learn my opinion on such matters. Recently, however, a news article crossed my path that really got me thinking, and as it was parenting-related, I decided to add a little vent about it. My apologies in advance.

The other day, I read a news story reporting a child somewhere in the United States who was expelled from school for creating a page on a social networking Web site pretending to be his school's principal and saying "he"—in the first person, as the principal—was gay, into sex with boys, and so on. The kid was caught and expelled.

Here's where the story goes pear-shaped.

The parents are now *suing the school district for violating the boy's right to free speech!* I am not kidding. First of all, to the boy's parents, you're possibly morons. Before you attempt to sue someone for something, you should at least understand what it is you're trying to sue them for. What your brat reportedly did has nothing to do with his free speech. One cannot, under the umbrella of free speech, represent something about a person as fact that is not proven to be fact or, for that matter, misleadingly represent oneself as that person. Getting in trouble for doing these things does not violate the speaker's freedom of speech; it prevents people from slandering others, thus robbing them of *their* rights. Ever notice how news articles always say someone has "allegedly" done something until a jury finds them guilty? It's only at that point the news outfits are allowed to drop the word "allegedly." You are, I allege, idiots and possibly criminally stupid.

Secondly, what exactly are you trying to teach your child here? Your kid—allegedly—did something wrong. Very, very wrong. Is the right lesson to teach him here that you'll bail him out anytime he slanders someone or breaks some law or that by going to the press and filing some ridiculous lawsuit he can get himself out of any jam? Maybe, and I'm just spit-balling here, you should focus instead on the idea that what he—allegedly—did was wrong and what he—allegedly—did was slander someone, someone who's probably getting paid way too little trying to turn your little shit into a productive member of society (which, given his apparent lineage, might just be impossible). And your little turd—allegedly—did it in an attempt to ruin the principal's career—one that the principal no doubt spent his entire adult life cultivating. No, no, you're—allegedly—fine with your kid ruining a professional educator's life for the sole purpose of his own amusement, as long as he doesn't get kicked out of school for it. Ridiculous.

This is such a sad commentary on our society. I don't think I'm overstating things when I say this is one of the key problems with how we Americans live day to day. We're always looking for how we've been wronged and who can pay us for it. Why can't we all take responsibility for our own lives? Why is it we always seem to be looking for someone to pay us off, even for our own mistakes or transgressions?

Again, going back to the "when I was a kid" frame, if I had done something akin to this as a youth, the good old-fashioned beat-down I would've received from my mom would've resulted in permanently slurred speech. And my mom was pretty easygoing. And she would've been right. Come on folks, let's keep our eye on the ball here.

What exactly are we trying to prepare our kids for in their adulthood, and what kind of world do we want them creating and living in? They'll be the ones taking care of us when we need our diapers changed, remember? We have a responsibility to instill in our children certain understandings of right and wrong, good and bad, and of just plain old personal responsibility. Being our children's best friends and rescuing them from any trouble they willingly get themselves into shouldn't be our first priority. Making sure they know the difference between right and wrong and want to choose the former over the latter should be our first priority. Making sure they don't constantly require rescuing and helping them understand that when they do screw up, there are consequences should also be a top priority. Moral backbones don't just magically appear in the next generation; they're built and forged by us, the ones who should be leading by example.

While I'm at it, so the aforementioned alleged morons don't sue me, I will suggest here that I probably made that story up and that any similarity between my story and real events chronicled in the news or other public forums at any point is purely coincidental.

# 35

## *And So We Come to the End of Trimester Number Two*

This week marked the end of the second trimester for Lucy and myself. Looking back, it was pretty much a period of nonactivity, especially for me. I'm not really sure what I expected, but it was definitely something more than what I found. I'm hoping that doesn't mean I've missed something big and obvious.

On the other hand, the past fourteen weeks were definitely interesting and filled with some pretty exciting milestones. The first time we saw our baby through an ultrasound actually looking like a baby was nothing short of awe-inspiring. Finding out "it" was a "she" was also a truly stunning moment. Lucy's also started looking pregnant, and the baby has made sure her presence is known with tiny little kicks, which, relative to her size, are probably pretty strong.

As long as I'm on the subject, I will draw the reader's attention to the fact that, early on in this chronicle, I mentioned that I never considered for a moment that we were having a boy, that I was 100 percent convinced it was going to be a girl from the time Lucy first told me as I got out of the shower on that Thursday morning. I don't know why I felt this way about it, but I did. I wish I could say it was some sort of connection to our unborn baby, but I think I'd be just trying to fool myself. Whatever the reason, I can definitely say "*Boo-yeah!* I was right! In your face—uh, someone!"

As I said before, we already know what our daughter's name will be. I won't tell you here, but I will say that I managed to pick out the middle name myself and get a stamp of approval from the wife on it.

Also, and this is particularly cool, the middle name is inspired by a Rush song. And it's not even a contrived one (like "Sawyer" or "Bytorina" or "Cygnus-ella"—hyphens added to aid the reader in recognizing the actual song titles) for the sole purpose of being able to use a Rush song that would end up being odd and ostracizing in a way discussed in my earlier rant about names. It's actually quite nice. You'll find out in about nineteen weeks.

I am somewhat concerned, however, that little in the way of true preparation has really happened yet. We haven't painted or prepared the nursery. We haven't begun collecting a mountain of gadgets, gizmos, and fluffy things for the baby, and we haven't registered for gifts. About the only thing we've done aside from our doctor's visits is get frustrated beyond reason while trying to decide on a stroller. Oh, except that I have purchased all Phoenix Suns-related baby gear that I could get my hands on, so I guess that's a checkmark on the plus side. I'm still searching for a shirt that says *Suns fan from birth* and another that says *Laker hater from birth*, but fortunately I have some time.

I'm hoping this period of nonactivity is a sign of things to come. If the next nineteen weeks go as the past ones have, this should be a no-brainer. Honestly, I don't know what everyone gets so excited about.

# PART FOUR

The Third Trimester: It's All Down Hill from Here (And Me with My Brakes Cut)

# 36

## *So That's How You Do It!*

I'm beginning to get worried about how little prep work for our coming daughter has been done thus far. It doesn't help that everyone I talk to starts out by asking excitedly, "So are you two getting ready? Are you almost done?" When I say we haven't really started, they all, as though reading from the same script, respond with, "Oh, well, that's no problem, you've got plenty of time, and there's really not that much to do anyway."

What the hell? If there's really not that much to do, why does everyone keep asking me if I'm done? I'm freaking out here. Does this make me a poor father already? (To my daughter, who will some day read this: If I'm a poor father now, I can only claim that it's my first try. I hope you can cut me a little slack and realize it's not that I don't care: I'm just a novice. If I'm a poor father later, I hope I have a new excuse. If you're screwed up in some big way, I doubt it's due to the fact I have yet to decide which car seat you'll be riding around in. Oh man, I hope.)

I am honestly beginning to feel there's some huge list of mission-critical to-dos we should be fulfilling every day and Lucy's GYNie simply forgot to include it in our forest-killing pile of crap to read. She probably thinks she put it there, but who can help missing a few pages in a stack like that? One day, we'll be in her office and she'll ask if we've gotten to number six hundred forty-seven on the list yet. Lucy and I will exchange nervous glances and respond with, "Uh, list? What list?" The doc will freak out, hand us a fifteen-page list in a three-ring binder, and tell us to get crackin', we've only got four weeks left.

The truth is, we try to get things moving, but we seem to run into walls that we can't move beyond until a certain stage in pregnancy. So, right now, we're focused on getting registered for the baby shower next month. That's progress, right? I think so. Trouble is, even for registering, there is a maze of stuff to run through—and really, where do you start?

I think we've got a system now: We have identified and ordered the crib as well as the related furniture. From there, we're branching out to bedding. Now that we know it's a girl, we can move on to some of the clothing. So for all of you out there looking for some advice, that's it: start with the crib and move out from there. Think of it like tossing a stone in a lake: move out from the center, and not just in terms of from the center of the baby's room, but from the center of the baby's daily activities. Crib for sleeping, furniture for storing stuff the baby will need when she wakes up, things to keep her occupied when out of the crib, things to ride in the car in when she leaves the house, and so on. (I'll let you know soon if this has actually worked for us.)

Like the masochists we have always been, we made another attempt at getting a demo of strollers. We went to a fourth store for this purpose. (Note: At the end of the last chapter, I mentioned a friend suggested we go without a stroller. Lucy and I decided that, for our purposes, this is a good idea and one we plan to employ. However, Lucy brought up the fact that there definitely will be times when we want to go for a casual stroll or will need to be holding something while we have the baby. In these scenarios, a stroller is a better approach. So we're going for a combined strategy.) This store was completely different from the other three in one key way: people were actually helpful. Seizing upon a salesperson that apparently hadn't yet gotten the memo instructing her to ignore all customers, we secured a demo of two different strollers: the hugely complex, yet simple-looking one I tried at the first store and a second one that another person I know swears by.

We tried the second one first. I was amazed at how heavy this thing was. No kidding, it was twenty-seven pounds unladen. I couldn't believe the manufacturers didn't see an issue with this. Note to manufacture: not all women out there are looking to tone up while stowing baby strollers in the trunks of their cars. Plus, even when fully compacted, it was still bulky. Lucy quickly decided the better of it, and we wandered over to the simple-looking, yet annoyingly complex one from the first store we visited.

I loved how this fine young salesperson made short work out of collapsing the stroller that I and seven other men had struggled with for many long, painful minutes. A click here, two presses here, and a tap there and it fell to the ground—collapsed like a deflated balloon. I was just waiting for her to end her demo with, "Only a top-shelf, grade-A dipshit couldn't do this in one try." Watching her though, no matter how many times she described it as, "really easy," as she went, I felt like I was watching a baseball manager sending in signals to a base runner. I began to think it was like a safe combination. They made it tough to ensure the only person who can work it was the rightful owner. Once collapsed, she showed me how easily it could be made usable again. Sure enough, in just slightly under seven seconds, it was back up and on four wheels. (It would've been three seconds, but she lost time pointing and narrating her activity.)

Now my turn was up, and I was feeling the pressure to perform. She had me start out by trying to pop open a newly re-collapsed stroller. I pressed the two buttons the saleslady had shown me, raised the handle, grabbed the bar, and pulled up. When she did this, the stroller popped to life like a jack-in-the-box. When I did it, however, it did nothing but stay compressed. I stood there with the entire still-collapsed contraption dangling from my hand. Damn it. "Oh, you didn't press *both* buttons," she said. Oops, my bad. I set the still-deflated stroller back to first position and tried again. Same result. I'm telling you, I pressed the damn buttons.

Attempt three seemed to be going better. I could tell that I had both buttons pressed, as they made a click sound, and the handle came up as it did for her. So far, so good. Now I put my foot on the lower of two bars as instructed and lifted up on the middle bar. When I did, my foot got wedged between the two bars, which hurt like a bitch.

I got it on the fourth attempt. I was definitely getting worried I was in for a world of hurt here. Anyway, I finally got that little demon figured out (I tried it twice more: two more successes and no additional injuries), so I was feeling better about it by the time we left, but I was daunted by what a pain in the ass it was. I had no idea why these things, no matter which brand, had to be so complex, but all the literature made it sound like the easiest thing I'd ever do. Why couldn't they be honest? Tell me in the pamphlet that was going to be a bitch to operate but it was also safe as hell, and once I figured it out, I'd never forget. Plus, let me know that, once I understood it, I'd jump up a few points on an IQ test. Take that approach and I'd have signed up for whatever classes that might have been needed to master it. It's all about setting expectations early. All I could say after was, my friggin' toe hurt from the stupid thing.

Summarized advice for the stroller: Don't take anyone's word on which stroller to get. Go out and give them a test drive, as these things need to really fit your personal requirements, especially regarding weight and size.

# 37

## *Illogical Concerns, Baby Showers, and You*

Our first third-trimester doctor's appointment came and went without significant changes in process or concerns. The same pattern played out as though we were on a rerun of a sitcom (a short one with no laugh track but still the same goofy character making sarcastic comments constantly—I will be playing that role in this episode). Despite the repetitive nature of these visits, they were definitely proving helpful for one key thing: in the time leading up to the visits, Lucy would begin to worry something had gone wrong with our little daughter, and these visits—specifically when the doctor listened to the baby's heartbeat—were becoming an excellent way to reassure her that all was still going well.

Part of the reason Lucy worried about problems, apart from it just being natural to do so, was that we purchased one of those home baby heartbeat monitors. This was basically just a microphone in a nice package with volume control and with headphones. Do yourselves a favor and don't get these before the third trimester. After opening the box, we found the directions actually said the earliest one stood a chance of being able to hear the heartbeat through that device was the first week of the third trimester. Of course, the only way to read that helpful little bit was to buy one, open it, and read the instructions. (Well, for us that was the case. For you, the reader, consider yourself clued in.)

So, even though we knew it was too early as soon as we opened the box, we set about periodically trying to hear the heartbeat and were, of course, constantly disappointed. Apparently, we believed ours was some sort of superbaby with a hyper-sonorous heart. As we got closer and closer to the end of the second trimester, we tried more frequently but still did not achieve success. While theoretically we knew this was normal, it did add just a bit of fuel to Lucy's concerns about the baby. Fortunately, these bouts of concern often seemed to coincide with visits to the GYNie, so I didn't worry too much about it. We'd be hearing that sound soon enough. At the office, this rhythmic music always immediately relaxed Lucy.

So for all you pregnant worriers or significant others of pregnant worriers; take it easy on these devices. Feeling the baby moving around is a much better indicator that all's well than hearing the heart (or failing to) is. Having said that, once you reach the third trimester, it *is* nice to have. We heard the baby's heartbeat tonight for the first time independent of a trip to the GYNie.

At this time, plans for the baby shower are coming along swimmingly. I can say that because I have no input in them whatsoever. Apparently, it's pretty important that men aren't involved. It seems if men had to organize baby showers, they'd all be held in one of the guys' basements, set around the pool table, and catered by the best pizza that can be delivered in less than thirty minutes. And every one of us would be shocked when our ladies were bothered by these plans. (We're not trying to be "guys" or slobs or anything, we just see celebrations as *the simpler the better*. As long as it gets the job done, mission accomplished. No?)

Anyway, the main baby shower (also known as the one with family) will be held in Denver next month. Lucy's done her part for it by sending the invitations and scouting the location on line. Everything is now in the hands of her family to drive it home. I have no idea what exactly goes on at these things, and I hope I never do. I'm still hoping to be playing poker with her uncles and male cousins that day.

Recently, however, our friends locally indicated they wanted to hold a party here so they could all share in this time with us. (This was not altogether unexpected but still very cool. Our friends rock.) Lucy's immediate reaction was to say no. Lucy has always been concerned with other people's feelings about things and worried that folks might only go to our baby shower out of obligation and also worried that asking people for gifts was presumptuous and rude. I tried (finally successfully) to explain that people actually enjoyed these things and that they really did want to be a part of this whole experience. This was a way for them to share in a great event with us. She finally capitulated by saying we could have said party if it were a "party" and not a "shower." (The key difference here being it was to be couples instead of ladies only, and she was hoping people did not feel compelled to bring gifts.) One of our best friends, Big Mike, was to helm the barbeque, and it would be more of a party than anything else. All we were going to have to do was work on the guest list. Seemed like a good deal to me.

So now we have two parties to look forward to. If I can register for basketball gear, this could really turn out to be a boon for me. I wonder if I can convince folks that the PS3 on the registry is for our daughter? We may need to have more kids.

Unrelated note: Another person asked me today if we're ready. Damn it! What do these people know that we don't, and why the hell aren't they sharing it with me?

# 38

# *Baby Registries, Odd Movements, and Basketball Games*

It's a week to the day since my last update. This puts us coming in at week twenty-seven.

We continue to make progress on the baby registry. This is becoming more and more important as time goes by because invitations to the shower have already been sent. Lucy now tells me there are already two purchases from the list. Yep, we need to get crackin'.

This is tough because there really aren't that many of the big-ticket necessities that we can register for, and even fewer of these under, say, a few hundred bucks, are out there, which we would feel pretentious registering for. The stroller is on the list, however, coming in at $900. (I don't really expect anyone to get that for us but heck, if they really want to, who am I to say no?) So the registry list is short. It's actually shorter than the expected list of attendees at the main baby shower. Now we feel like we have to add stuff, but we're just running out. It's not unlike when we were doing our wedding registry and we kept adding place settings or sets of sheets.

Lucy, understandably, doesn't want to put baby clothes on the list, as folks are likely to get those anyway. We've listed the basics, the next-in-line basics, and a modest list of this-would-be-cool items. Still, I feel under-registered. I'm not trying to be a snot here. I really feel people are going to want to participate in outfitting our little tyke, and I very much appreciate it; I am just having a bit of trouble enabling that to happen in a way Lucy feels is conducive to our room's décor without her feeling like a heel for "asking" for.

I'm also shying away from putting any toys on the list. I figure it's probably going to be several months before our little girl is aware enough of her surroundings to need toys to keep her stimulated (i.e., quiet). I'm not sure about the timing of that, but I suspect there's time to make the toy thing happen appropriately.

Earlier in the week we saw our daughter's movement firsthand and unaided by technology. It was the first time I saw Lucy's belly twitch. It was pretty cool seeing the baby move around like that. I was recently told there would be a point when we'd be able to see full shifting of the baby like painting on a canvass. Someone told me we'd be able to see outlines of hands and feet through Lucy's stomach. This was some pretty cool stuff, but it may also gross me out a bit going forward.

On a totally unrelated and annoying note: the Suns lost game one of the playoffs today. What's worse, they lost to the Spurs. I hate the Spurs almost as much as I hate the Lakers. Damn. I could've used this win to brighten up the ol' day.

# 39

## *All Right, I Did It. But I'm Not Ashamed. Okay, Maybe a Little.*

We played music for our unborn daughter today. Yes, I admit it, we put the speaker right on Lucy's belly and gave our baby-in-progress her first taste of Rush (the song that inspired her middle name).

Lots of people play music for their unborn babies because they think it will stimulate the baby's brain development. I don't know if that's true, as nobody has yet been able to actually prove or disprove the theory, but I figure, what the hell, couldn't hurt. (Never met a bandwagon I didn't like.) Whether or not it stimulates her brain development, if it gives her a taste for really good music and a loathing for crap music, I figure it'll be worth the time invested and internal embarrassment that results.

So today Rush, later classical. People always say to play classical music for the baby, but I bet precious few of the people who say that actually listen to classical music themselves. It's as if they're hoping their kids will magically have better taste than they, the parents, do. I don't think there's anything wrong with that plan, but it is an interesting commentary. So every successive generation should have better taste than the one before. Good plan. Eventually, there would be no more country music to speak of. Nothing wrong with that. I actually do like classical and jazz, though, so I will be forcing my tastes on our daughter. However, I am staying away from Mozart, Handel, and anything with a harpsichord. I figure it's got to be Tchaikovsky if we're going to do classical. (Nothing with cannon fire, though.)

# 40

## *My God, What Have They Done to Us?*

I play basketball three times a week: Monday and Wednesday nights and Saturday mornings. Each session has pretty much the same crowd of men—all guys trying desperately to hang on to their youths or playing a sound track in their heads of, "Three—two—he shoots ... *he scores! The* (enter favorite team name here) *win!*" with every pull-up jumper they attempt. It's just twenty or so men running around with far too much testosterone flowing, all secretly hoping that one day an NBA scout just happens by, sees them, and decides that they're just what the Warriors have been needing all this time.

Conversations between and following games typically center around who did what at which bar with how hot a chick, how much beer they consumed last weekend, or what Kobe or LeBron did the night before.

After this morning's session, however, I had the most unusual experience. In the locker room afterward, three of us stood around—clothed, I will add—and talked about babies, our wives being pregnant, preparing for the arrival, and so on. We talked for forty-five minutes. Who the hell turned us into women while we slept?

# 41

## *Oh Yeah, Well, Your Mother Dresses You Funny!*

Week twenty-nine was upon us. Apart from taking a short trip home to Phoenix to visit my family, there was not too much exciting about it. This was the first time my family had seen Lucy actually looking pregnant, so everyone was pretty excited to take note of my wife's circumference.

Once there, my three nieces eagerly huddled up around Lucy to get a feel of the belly, hoping for that ever so exciting kick, twitch, or shift from our daughter. They stood around Lucy like her belly was the Stanley Cup and they all wanted to keep their hands on it. It took a while, but our little girl finally obliged them with a kick here or there.

It was in Phoenix that Lucy first noticed some of the current pregnancy-related unpleasantries. Her ankles were swollen and her sciatic nerve was killing her. (The latter is more commonly known as; her ass was hurting.)

Also in Phoenix this trip, I found someone to make the *Suns fan from birth* and *Laker hater from birth* shirts for my little girl, so bonus!

Lately, I'd begun noticing people tended to think the strangest things were compliments to a pregnant woman. In our favorite restaurant the other day, one of the waitresses looked at Lucy and said, "*Wow!* You're getting so *big!*" Maybe I was in left-field on this one, but I thought if I, or any other human, said that to any nonpregnant woman, we'd have heard about it on the news with a lead-in that started, "Tragedy struck in a small restaurant today."

Yet, oddly, because Lucy was with child, this was supposed to be a compliment or, at least, not offensive. This was slightly less annoying than the strangers who would come up asking to feel Lucy's belly (what is that all about?), but still just so strange. I would've died a happy man if Lucy had replied, "*Wow!* You still don't shower regularly."

Oh yeah, the number of people this week who have asked me if we're ready: three.

# 42

## *So What You're Saying Is, We Should Actually Do What You're Telling Us?*

Week thirty starts out with a regular trip to the GYNie. It's the last of our monthly visits. Going forward, visits will be twice-monthly then moving to weekly during the last month until D-day.

With this trip to the GYNie comes newfound anxiousness about how little we've done in the way of anything resembling preparation. Unlike before, where the anxiety was due to the lack of any tasks at hand, this time we know of some things that really need to be done and we just haven't been able to find the time for yet. For example, when the doctor asks whether we've found a pediatrician yet, we haven't; we haven't really looked yet.

At the same time, some of the baby gifts have started arriving. This is kind of neat but is also anxiety-inducing as it reminds us that we not only have no place to store these things right now, we don't really have anywhere to store the actual baby yet. Lucy is working on the spare room, and considering where it was when she started, she's moved mountains. Now, however, the bed is overflowing with crap we have to find a place for. Also, the closet needs to be emptied of the wall of crap that now occupies it.

The thirty-week visit to the doctor also comes with an ultrasound. Once again, everything is looking pretty good. The only concern from the visit is that Lucy's still not really gaining any weight. As a result, the GYNie explains the baby's midsection is "lagging a bit" in terms of growth in comparison to the baby's head. Resisting the urge to make sarcastic comments about us bearing a real-life bobblehead doll (it wasn't easy), Lucy and I begin plotting out ways she can gain the requested pound-per-week. It is odd that this particular instruction from the doctor is met with a heavy sigh from the wife. I would've thought a doctor telling a woman to eat more and gain some weight is like a judge sentencing a kid to do jail time in a candy store. I think the issue here is that food just doesn't really have a big draw for Lucy right now. She's still coming down off the period of constant indigestion and heartburn, so food isn't quite what it used to be for her. We're working out a snack menu that will include nuts, cheeses, and crackers she can snack on during the day at work. The key, we've been informed, is to eat snacks throughout the day. Hopefully, in two weeks, Lucy will be two pounds heavier and our little girl's midsection will be back up to par.

Also, at this stage in the baby book we've been reading, I found a short list of many things that might physically and emotionally irritate the mother. For example: Lucy dreamed last night that I was married to another woman (not in lieu of Lucy, along with Lucy) and she was arguing with me about what irritated the other wife. And, coincidentally, earlier today I saw in the book that we have entered a time we could expect she may start having some odd dreams, so right on target there.

In fact, reading through the list of maladies and general oddities that may happen to a woman during this time, I find Lucy's been complaining about around 80 percent of them. Fortunately, she hasn't yet gotten hemorrhoids or constipation. Aside from those, she's like a poster child for crap that's going to happen to irritate a pregnant woman. There should be a poster of her in the GYNie's office with little arrows point to various parts of her anatomy with labels like, "Will bloat" or "This is going to hurt" or "Will change colors" or, pointing to her head, "Will become even more difficult to understand than before."

We're getting ready to head back to Denver this weekend for the baby shower and Mother's Day. This is going to be the first time any of her family will see her since Christmas, so as with my family, it will be the first time any of them see her actually looking pregnant.

The various cramps, swollen parts, aches, and pains associated with being thirty-weeks pregnant should really amplify the earlier mentioned mental issues she has about Denver, so it's going to pretty much be a party for me. As another milestone, this will be the last trip we can take before the baby arrives. (Airlines and doctors won't let a woman fly beyond thirty-two or so weeks of pregnancy, apparently fearing in-flight births. Personally, I think they're missing a golden opportunity to get some press time for positive stuff.)

From this point forward, it's single-digit weeks countdown. Definitely starting to get a little nervous now.

# 43

## *Braxton-Hicks Was a Jerk!*

The day before Mother's Day was set for our family baby shower in Denver. We arrived in Denver on Friday evening and met up with my mother and sister, who decided to fly in and attend. Given that it was May, which would translate to sunshine and warmth everywhere else, it was, of course, windy, overcast, and snowing in Denver. What a crappy place (as my wife reminded me constantly).

At the shower, I was the only male amongst forty-five attendees. Great fun. My job that morning was to record the event and take pictures. No problem. As long as I didn't have to participate in any of the reindeer games, I was fine with it. The games themselves were pretty innocuous, but the one where each table nominated one of the women to be "pregnant" while the others found the most outrageous way to turn a plain white T-shirt into "maternity wear" was downright scary. I realize these fine, upstanding women being totally satirical and intentionally outrageous, but all I can say is the winner ended up being the lady walking around, feigning drunk, with a pair of little pink baby booties tied to her crotch (representing the baby on the way out—breech, I might add), totally ridiculous drawings on the shirt, cigar hanging out of her mouth, and a drink in one hand. Again, I realize this was a joke, but don't they say all jokes are formed from a grain of truth? Was I possibly witnessing a bit of flashback from these ladies—all older than Lucy and I—rearing their children?

Remind me to keep away from whatever book on child raising comes from that table.

At the party, we received plenty of cute, soft, plush you-name-its. I think we've now got everything we need except for a baby, something to carry it in, something to strap it into when in the car, and someplace to put it when it sleeps. Other than that, we're set.

A couple days later, Lucy and I were having dinner at a party thrown by her uncle. The party was a get-together for the entire clan to spend time with Lucy's great-aunt and uncle, who were visiting for the baby shower.

About halfway through dinner, Lucy's entire midsection tightened up and seized on her. She sat there, not daring to move, for many minutes. Not wanting to call undue attention to her, possibly resulting in needless worry for all those around, I tried to comfort her rather discreetly. For about five minutes, Lucy was rendered almost unable to move. Or, at least, unable to move without excruciating pain.

Lucy was experiencing what we had been warned would be coming our way: Braxton-Hicks contractions. Turns out, these were fairly common and just one more way this entire pregnancy thing sucks for women. Named after the doctor who first figured out what was going on, Lucy's GYNie told us Braxton-Hicks contractions were a woman's entire midsection contracting in a process of, essentially, practicing giving birth.

I had no idea human bodies could take it upon themselves to practice anything involuntarily. I suppose a woman's body would take it upon itself to practice because no right-minded person would have ever practiced such a thing on her own. This really sucked for Lucy. It was as though 30 percent of her body was going into rigor mortis while the remaining 70 percent shouted at the first 30 percent, "What the hell are you doing?" Finally, it subsided, but it was really an uncomfortable moment—for her, physically, for me, just because there was, as always, nothing I could do. Very strange.

The rest of the week in Denver went without incident. There was plenty of complaining about Denver coming from my wife's direction, but all things considered, the trip was a good one. Our final pre-parental flight home went without issue except for the couple sitting behind us, whose child insisted on screaming at random intervals. Not screaming in that "I've hurt myself" or "I'm hungry" sort of way but screaming in that "Hey, it's much too quiet on this plane right now, maybe I should let out a bloodcurdling scream to break the tension" sort of way. When not screaming, the child could be seen running up and down the aisle, getting under foot of the flight attendants, who somehow managed to restrain themselves from stuffing said child into the overhead bin. (It was full.)

Realizing I've made many earlier rants on examples of various styles of parenting, I won't comment further on this one except to say the flight sucked until I was able to fish some loud, angry music (Tool) out of my backpack and go to my happy place.

In short, another great trip visiting her family. Talking with my friends and colleagues from time to time, I realize just how lucky I am to have her family as my in-laws. I've heard what other people go through. My wife's family is just great. All of them. I wish there was a way to have them all come out here to be with us when the baby arrives. It would be great to have everyone around. Unfortunately, apart from it being nearly impossible to arrange such a thing logistically, Lucy might break my kneecaps if I merely suggest it, so I think I'll leave that subject alone.

# 44

## *Our Baby's First Hardware*

During our thirty-second week of pregnancy (well, Lucy's—I'm just along for the ride), we had another appointment with the GYNie. In the two weeks since the last one, Lucy gained a pound. The doctor was hoping for two. Doc wasn't overly bothered about this, but I felt like she told us in a disappointed tone. You know, not actually saying, "Hey man, get off the pot and make something happen here," but probably thinking it very clearly. It has been tough for Lucy as she really hasn't had any sort of appetite since the Indigestion Age. Lucy promised to get on the dime and make some big gains (no pun intended—okay, maybe a little) going forward.

The visual part of things was really heating up too. While lying back on the couch the other night, Lucy's stomach was constantly shifting, poking out, and whatnot. All in all, it was getting quite exciting around here.

Preparations are continuing on the spare room. Somehow, though, even more crap has accumulated since Lucy made her first attempt to organize and clean. I don't understand how that happens, but it certainly does suck. I truly have no idea where this stuff is going to go. (And I'm not even talking about baby stuff here. This is all *our* crap.) The mound of stuff has now grown from "pile" to "hill." Not quite a "mountain," but if we don't get it under control, we'll soon be there.

I've made a small but noticeable dent in the heap of crap. Anything that is obviously a *get rid of* or a *for donation* item has been moved to a separate pile for easy future disposal. So what I've realized is that we have so much crap we need to categorize it. Nuts.

As of today, we are finally in possession of the baby's first piece of post-birth hardware. The crib is now fully assembled in what will be the sleeping quarters. We are stunned at how huge it is. It is ridiculously large. Even in a room that is more than fairly good sized, it just doesn't fit. It consumes the room. It doesn't help that there's also a queen-sized bed in the room, which we're keeping since this room is still going to be the spare room for guests when needed. The crib is so large that there is barely eighteen inches of clearance between it and the edge of the bed. This simply won't do. It's so close; we can't open the crib drawer on the bottom. Hell, we can't even *install* the crib drawer. I have no idea what we're going to do here.

My solution is to put it next to the bed, which would necessitate moving the bed to the left about two feet. Lucy quickly dismisses this solution with a look on her face that I would expect to see if someone ever suddenly runs up and just hands her a pile of dog crap. "There is *no* way I can handle having the bed off center on the wall. No way."

My problem here is, I'm a guy. For me, this is a workable solution in a temporary situation. (We're planning on moving next spring, so this solution would be for less than a year.) I'm pretty sure any guy out there would agree with me on this. The crib will fit, the bed will fit, you can move around the room, and you can access all needed storage areas. Problem solved. Lucy doesn't care. This means we are now in negotiations with the laws of physics to get this crib designed for a bear cub to work in a way allowed by the laws of aesthetics. (The only rule I've set is that Lucy is prohibited from making it work in any way that employs a chain saw.)

# 45

## *What Happened to All the Stuff? Oh, There It Is.*

On the Friday of our thirty-third week (as it relates to the pregnancy, we count weeks from Wednesday to Tuesday), I was planning on going to my friend's house for a poker tournament. Before I left, Lucy asked if I could help her reorient the queen-size bed. Not to go into full diagrams to describe Lucy's solution, but suffice it to say it involved turning the bed sideways so it would still fit along the center of the wall and then rearranging some of the accompanying furniture. I said I thought it was going to look weird having a bed oriented sideways along the middle of a wall but, being a guy, she didn't care what I thought on matters of aesthetics.

Mind you, there was still a voluminous amount of stuff in this room. Shelves that were once full of crap now stood empty and waiting to be moved to the garage, and the stuff that was once on those shelves was piled up on the bed, desk, or floor.

Again, I was not exactly sold on the idea of reorienting the bed, but I wanted to be a team player here (and I was in no mood to argue with a pregnant woman), so I agreed to assist. Plus, if I didn't assist, Lucy would have done it on her own and likely hurt herself. Lucy claimed this layout for the room is just for the moment anyway, to allow her enough space to move around and clean. So we moved the bed, which was incredibly difficult because:

1.  It fit almost perfectly in the space is was currently occupying with all of the crap and the crib that surrounded it and

116

2. I wasn't allowed to move the bed in any way that either knocked over the piles of stuff or dinged the walls or surrounding furniture.

After the bed was moved, I prepared to leave for my game and, knowing Lucy would try to make tremendous strides on the room after I left, I asked her numerous times not to move or lift anything heavy or awkward after I left. (The one bit of nagging I get to do is chastising her for lifting or moving anything that might result in hurting herself. It's the only thing I've got, so I jump on it.) She promised—most exasperatedly—that she wouldn't, and I departed.

The poker tournament lasted until around 1:00 AM (I came in third thanks to a very, very poor call on my part), and I trekked home. Heading upstairs, I looked in the baby's room and found it completely done and organized, save for the alcove off the back, which serves as my office and library. The bed was now made with the new accoutrements procured to match the baby's bedding, and the various pieces of furniture, including a desk and other sundries, had been moved. The room, in all honesty, looked great. I doubt the bed will remain oriented sideways as it is, but the room certainly looks good enough to show off to anyone coming by asking, "So are you ready?"

One thing struck me suddenly though: what had happened to the piles and hills of stuff that had occupied this room just six hours earlier? As I came in, I noticed some of it had migrated to the garage, but that couldn't account for more than 15 to 20 percent of the total volume. I went to bed with the mystery still on my mind. The next morning, when I inquired how she got it done, Lucy promised me she managed to do all the work on the room without lifting anything heavy or struggling. I looked at her incredulously, not believing for a moment that she did not strain herself, and considered digging a bit deeper into the logistics. I have always tried not to call bullshit on my wife too often, though, so I elected to move on and instead went to play basketball. After I got back, I went into the room we use as our media room and found I literally couldn't walk into the room due to all the crap now occupying every square inch of horizontal space. I realized then the baby's room was completed at the expense of the media room. Essentially, it was cleaning by relocation. Excellent. (When I was a kid, I'd get in trouble if I cleaned my room in this manner. This is likely to be the first in a long line of double standards that await my daughter as she goes through life. Once again I say to her as she reads this some day, "Sorry, sweetie. Nothing I can do about it. Suck it up.")

# 46

## *Well, at Least Somebody's Amused*

The rest of the thirty-third and thirty-fourth weeks of our pregnancy were unremarkable except for the birthing class Lucy and I took. This was, apparently, a new version of the Lamaze classes expecting couples used to take. The woman leading the class was, quite possibly, the nicest and most helpful woman on the planet, but she was not without her quirks. She was, to be blunt, very eccentric and loud and one of those people who is perfectly comfortable talking to you while in your personal space. A direct transplant from 1960s Haight/Ashbury San Francisco, she was into all things granola, Zen, and flowery.

She also loved to make one-liners and follow them with bellowing fake laughs, which caused everyone to respond with that uncomfortable watching-a-stand-up-comic-die-on-stage sort of courtesy laugh. These evenings were sprinkled with random anecdotes from her work with couples, each one followed by a not-really-funny one-liner ending with her standing up straight, feet shoulder-width apart, and fists on her hips in classic Superman style, going, "HA HAAAAAA!" The sound was exactly that of the laugh from Wayland Flowers voicing his Madame puppet, only ten times louder. If I, or anyone else, said anything funny or anything that was merely *intended* to be funny, she would give the same response, only with her head back, no fists on hips, and a much longer series of, "HA HA HA HA HA HAAAAAA!" Sometimes, if I was lucky, she would lean down and do the laugh right in my face.

I, as I have mentioned, have always been a sarcastic bastard and occasionally have found so many zingers flying around my brain that one or two have slipped out despite my best intentions. After awhile, I stopped trying to keep them in and resorted to saying them just barely loud enough for Lucy to hear. Occasionally, one of the couples right next to us would hear too, and they'd get a chuckle, so I figured I was giving a little something back.

At one point, the instructor was demonstrating differing techniques to help get through the initial labor pains and used me as an example of a helpful husband. (The irony of her using me for such a demonstration was not lost on me or Lucy, as we both know I cannot be helpful without adding my own commentary. Sure, I'll be helpful, but it'll cost ya!) She handed me one end of a rope with a handle on both sides, and she took the other. The exercise—which, I will add, seems like it will be genuinely helpful—involved me holding on to the rope for support with her at the other end leaning back, knees bent with feet shoulder-width apart, and swaying a bit. Of course, as only a child such as I would do, I did a fake let-go of the rope as our instructor was leaning back, and she, for just a moment, got that, "Oh shit!" look of surprise on her face before realizing I hadn't actually let go of the rope. She quickly recovered her wits and peppered me with a lengthy blast of, "HA HA HA HA HA HA HA HAAAAAA!" quite literally getting the last laugh.

Along with some genuinely helpful instruction on dealing with labor and things related to birthing, there was quite a bit of good advice provided on how to prepare, what to pack for the hospital, signs to look for in labor, and so on. Honestly, this was a very helpful class, and I was glad we took it. From that point on, we were focused on getting Lucy's bag filled up with the things she'll need for the big day. I decided classes of this nature are great, and I definitely planned on recommending them.

There was also one couple taking copious notes on *everything* the instructor said, as though every noun and verb was a potential gold nugget that would render the birthing process a nonevent for them. They wrote everything down. Did they think they would be able to leaf through their notes during the delivery like some sort of NFL football coach sending in signals to the QB? I was suddenly picturing the husband wearing one of those forearm bands NFL QBs wear, crouched in huddle position next to the wife's hospital bed, flipping up the cover during contractions to work out the next play. "Look honey, I'm gonna need you to keep it together on this next contraction now, you're really embarrassing yourself with all this yelling and screaming.

Okay, ready? We're going wide-left, bear down, straight for the end-zone here and don't forget your breathing!"

Also, they asked questions. Lots of them. They asked at least four questions to every one point the instructor made, and they asked even the most basic question as seriously as though their very existence depended on knowing the *official* answer to a question (Questions, I might add, that anyone with the power of rational thought would already know the answers to.) In an earthquake preparedness class, they would be the ones asking, pens poised above notepad to feverishly write down the response, "Okay, so during an earthquake, is it a good idea to watch out for things falling on you from shelves or other high places?" Everyone out there knows a guy like this. Now, imagine two of them, and they're married, and they're procreating. A real, no-kidding example came after the instructor had outlined some of the things that can be done to get labor to start up naturally (without drugs), which can, depending on the woman, include taking long walks, stretching, sex, and, in some cases, stimulating the nipples. Upon hearing the last one, the husband raised his hand and asked, "Exactly how much do you have to stimulate the nipples to cause her to go into labor?" There was no question in my mind that he had interpreted the instructor's comment to mean that if his wife is in her eighth to ninth month of pregnancy and she merely brushed something across a nipple, say, when toweling off after a shower, she would have to be mindful of where she walked as she just might step on her newly delivered baby. Once they crossed the thirty-six-week threshold, he would probably be reminding her each morning when she got in the shower, "Watch out for your nipples!"

Also during these two weeks, we had our local baby party for some of our friends here in the Bay Area. Earlier in this journal, I mentioned that we had decided not to tell anyone the baby's name, given the annoying tendency of humans to interject their opinions on such matters. Well, that didn't last. Lucy decided I was nuts or, at least, overly secretive, and started telling everyone. I decided, hell, the cat's out of the bag, I might as well play along, so I also told folks. Fortunately, whether folks like the name or not, everyone very kindly at least pretended to—almost everyone, that is. During our baby shower party, I told a friend of mine's girlfriend our daughter's intended name.

She immediately crinkled up her nose and said, "Hmm, no. Nope, I don't like it. You should change it."

When I explained, in much nicer terms than I was thinking, that despite her splendid (though unsolicited) opinion on the matter, we were not going to change the name, she told me we should at least spell it differently than we intended to. (Our daughter's name is pretty much made up, yet it's very similar to a more common name so we had to invent the spelling in such a way that anyone looking at it would be able to pronounce it correctly.) This girlfriend spent the next ten minutes telling me how wrong I was about this and that I really needed to listen to her.

I realized later my only real mistake here was not just getting up and walking away as she began shoving her opinion down my throat. Don't get me wrong, I appreciate that everyone has the right to their opinions and even the right to express them. However, one should be mindful of one's audience and keep an eye on the line between friendly unsolicited advice and refusal to let something drop when your opinion is noted yet not acted upon.

The party was otherwise uneventful and resulted in more various sundries for our baby. Big Mike manned the barbeque, and it was, quite possibly, the best I'd ever had. His prep work for the barbeque was in our kitchen, however, and the resulting mess had our kitchen looking like some redneck front yard where one might find an old rusting Buick. Maybe that's what's needed for truly good barbeque. The cleanup took something in the order of three hours.

# 47

## *Oh Great, More Sort-of Advice ... Exactly What We Needed!*

In a noteworthy change of approach, people have lately stopped asking me if we're ready for the arrival of our first child. I think everyone now just assumes we're not (a not unreasonable assumption). Now the question of our readiness has been replaced by a simple yet completely unhelpful piece of advice: get as much sleep as you can; soon you won't get any.

Again I say, thanks, but what exactly am I supposed to do with this? Are humans now able to save up sleep for future significantly deprived states? Do we stock up now and receive our sleep coupons in the mail, which we can cash-in on a particularly tough night? If I continue to save up for a while, will I suddenly fill up and not have to sleep at all for a week or two? I'm sure folks just say this as an attempt at humorous yet ominous foreshadowing and that they don't actually expect us to stock up in the sleep department, but it's just such an odd thing to say to someone.

A good friend of mine took this particular style of advice a bit further, though, and now I definitely think I'm in trouble. The conversation went like this:

Her: "Make sure you get your sleep now!"

Me: "I can't sleep now; I'm at lunch." (Mutual courtesy laugh) "Anyhoo, seriously, I'll try. You know what's funny? Everyone I talk with about the baby now—and I do mean *everyone*—warns me about the sleep thing."

Her: "But do they warn you 'bout the mustard poo and the diaper busters?"

Me: "Uh, 'scuse me?"

# 48

## *Heading into the Home Stretch*

The most notable thing about week thirty-five was just how much our daughter was moving around in her tiny little corner of her mommy. Numerous times this week, Lucy suddenly grabbed her side and winced in pain as our little girl stretched out and performed calisthenics.

After having dinner the other night, Lucy was suddenly in excruciating pain. I looked over to see a big lump sticking out of the right of her abdomen and another out the front. Our little girl might have been doing Pilates for all appearances. Carefully, I tried a soft rubbing motion to coax whatever our daughter was trying to stick through Lucy's side back to where it was supposed to be.

Today, Lucy again reeled in pain, and, resting a hand on her stomach, I felt a foot going under her rib cage. No fun, I am certain. Eventually, our daughter realized she could not break free of her prison directly through the walls and reverted to her attempts to tunnel out, which afforded Lucy a rest.

The other notable thing about week thirty-five was that it was week thirty-five out of forty. Our proximity to the finish line was hanging over us like a banner. As the days passed, I found myself growing more and more excited to meet our little girl. Lucy has again been napping quite a bit and going through periods of intense discomfort for obvious reasons. She was again having trouble sleeping at night, as that seemed to be when our little girl was trying the hardest to get in shape before she was born. The harder Lucy tried to sleep, the more the baby's movement level ratcheted up.

Like so many other stages of this process, I am left feeling there's little I can do to contribute. I give back rubs and the like, but for the most part, Lucy gets to handle this one all on her own. She's not eating as much as she "should" be, owing to all of the discomfort. All in all, the past week has not been the brightest of this entire saga, but nearing the finish line does bring a sense of excitement that helps take some of the edge off.

As we head in to week thirty-six, I'm hoping the momentum of the last month is enough to sling-shot Lucy through to the finish line with her wits and emotional stability in tact. I guess we'll find out soon enough.

# PART FIVE

## The Last Four Weeks …
## Oh, It's *On* Now!

# 49

## *Buckle In and Keep Your Hands and Feet inside the Vehicle at All Times*

We are in what is currently anticipated to be the last four weeks, also known as the "home stretch," and all bets are off at this point. Week thirty-six is that point in a normal and healthy pregnancy where, while it's not expected our daughter will be arriving "any minute now," each day brings us closer to the likelihood that the next day is "the one."

I know this sounds like simple and obvious math to anyone reading this, but the sudden realization that, while we're not supposed to officially cross over to parenthood for another four weeks, the only thing really holding us back are the whims of my wife's body. There's no guarantee that we'll get to keep to this nearly arbitrarily set schedule. There is a very real *possibility* it could be any day, even if the *probability* of it being tomorrow is still pretty low. My point is, the end is all of the sudden upon us, and it's both cool and freaky at the same time.

In the end, the next three-and-a-half weeks will probably go much the same way the preceding ones have: Lucy's uncomfortable and in some manner of pain nearly all the time, and I'm trying to keep my head down in case things start to fly. And yet, because we can't be totally confident in the actual delivery date, there's a nervous sort of electricity in the air. It's a very surreal way to go about one's day.

Imagine someone told you that on a certain day in nine months you're going to have a major operation. Huge. Actually, we think it'll be that day plus or minus a few, but we don't know for sure. It's going to hurt. You're going to make it through, but it's going to hurt like a son of a bitch. Oh yeah, and your entire life thereafter will be different. Then, as you get closer and closer to that date, they tell you, "Well, it's going to happen in the next month, but we're not going to tell you exactly when. All you need to know is that every day that passes increases the likelihood it will be the next day, but it's probably not going to be for a while. You'll know it when it happens though because you're going to suddenly be in excruciating pain and you're going to start gushing liquids out of various orifices. Now, go relax."

Let's not forget that, at thirty-eight weeks, they consider a baby full-term. Thirty-eight! That's only two weeks away. Babies arrive one to two weeks early routinely. If thirty-eight weeks is technically full-term, then week thirty-six shouldn't shock the doctors too much, I would think.

I suppose I may be making a bigger deal out of this than it warrants. After all, it's not like I wasn't aware that, eventually, Lucy's being pregnant would result in our having a baby. I think it's just the feeling of being at the very top of one hell of a roller coaster after all the clank-clank-clanking is done and you're in that three seconds of silence and calm before you plummet down. It's both electrifying and scary at the same time. When you're standing in line for the ride, you know you'll eventually be dropping at some ridiculous rate, but until you're actually just about to go over the top, what that means doesn't quite register. I'm excited about our daughter's arrival in that same sort of way. The fear of the unknown cannot overshadow how excited we are, but the mix of the two emotions is pretty awe-inspiring.

# 50

## *Oh, You Weren't Kidding? Sorry.*

Apart from this newfound appreciation for the calendar, week thirty-six also reminded us that we still had a bunch of to-dos to do. Sunday was dedicated to clearing out the garage to make room for the continuous relocation of the crap from the closet of the baby/spare room to allow for the influx of baby-items. Interestingly, the pregnancy book I've been reading said this week could be marked by changes in Lucy's overall demeanor. The nesting tendency becomes more pronounced and emotions can run short. Never has our book been more accurate than when we were cleaning out the garage.

Lucy has always been stubborn in a way unparalleled by another living being, but when cleaning, this always reached a different level of neurosis. When cleaning in preparation for a baby, her neurosis went off the chart.

We have a washer and dryer in our garage—as is often the case in parts of the country that gets no snow or excessive heat. In our case, next to said washer and dryer, we had accumulated a small amount of junk that really needed to be addressed. As I began moving the stuff from this section to the middle of the garage and arranging it into piles of "trash" and "trash we might want to keep or donate," Lucy grabbed a vacuum and began cleaning up where this assortment of crap had been. Vacuuming. The garage. By itself, this seemed an odd approach to cleaning, at least in this reporter's opinion, but then came, "Okay, now can you pull out the washer and dryer so I can vacuum behind and under them?" This *request* was made with a completely straight face.

I was, for a moment, at a loss for what to do. For a split second, I thought she might be kidding. Vacuuming *under* any object that was never designed or intended to be moved was a concept outside the cleaning logic that all men were programmed with at a DNA level. For a man, if it was on the ground, has never moved, and was never going to move, there was no need to clean under it. This was such a plain and simple idea it shouldn't need to be stated. There were not going to be Clean Police coming over to our house asking to see the underside of any of our appliances. Yet I knew if I argued with her on this, I would instigate an argument that would last far too long and ruin both of our moods for the night, and I would have still ended up losing. So I relented and moved the appliances.

The thoroughness with which Lucy vacuumed under and behind these appliances would have made Martha Stewart at her most anal shed a tear. It was like she was going for an award. However, it did not stop there. She then proceeded to vacuum next to and around the water heater and furnace. Once again, I was at a loss. By the end of cleaning just this section of our two-car garage, we were ninety minutes into a job that, in total, should have taken us about two to three hours. In other words, vacuuming this section of the garage—an act I still don't really understand the purpose of on many levels—added anywhere from 50 to 75 percent more time to an already arduous task on a day of the week meant for relaxing and drinking beer.

In the end, we finally finished rearranging and cleaning the garage, and somehow I managed not to say anything that would cause a fight or tears. You may think this a relatively small accomplishment, but considering how sarcastic I am, keeping my mouth shut was no easy task at all.

# 51

## *Real, No-Kidding Advice for Men Going through This*

In an unusually sound move on my part, I have started my own preparation for being out of the office during the baby's arrival. My advice to you: don't underestimate how much you need to prepare for your own being out. Also keep in mind that, while we don't like to think about it, we need to be prepared to be out for an unplanned amount of time in case anything goes wrong. Some jobs will make this harder than others, but we really need to not under-think this. When you really start to contemplate it, you'll be amazed at how much there is to do. Go through it methodically and plan it out. And do it sufficiently in advance, because you don't actually know when your baby is going to arrive.

For example, I'm in a management capacity within my company and deal with dozens of different organizations routinely. I realize now that I am going to need to alert no fewer than a hundred people that I'll be out of the office for two weeks when the baby begins her exodus from the womb. I also have an appreciation for how little time I will have to send each of these folks an e-mail alerting them to my going on leave once I get that nudge, shout, or call from Lucy. There's just no way I will have the time nor presence of mind to get it all done once the ball starts rolling downhill. Sure, I have talked with my staff and let them know what to do while I'm out, but there are just so many other little things to hand off, wind up, or put on hold, not to mention people to deal with, that, if I don't start preparing now, it could be disastrous for my boss once I leave—and therefore for me when I return.

When I really think about all I have to get ready, coupled with my new-found anxiety that the baby could come at any moment (even though she's not likely to), I begin to panic. So now I have begun the prep work: writing a series of *I'm going to be out for two weeks* e-mails, addressing them, and saving them in my draft folder; handing off reports to my staff; having some staff members accompany me to meetings they would not ordinarily attend so they can take them over for me; and various other things. It's sort of a what-if-I'm-hit-by-a-bus plan in action.

Now that I think about it, I find it odd that I have never seen any advice along these lines for expectant fathers. This is huge. The last thing in the world I want to be worried about when going through a long labor period with my wife is whomever I forgot to e-mail or who is going to handle that report for me while I'm out. I'm pretty sure I'd never be forgiven for logging in to drop some e-mails from Lucy's bedside while she's between contractions. Do they even have wireless in delivery rooms? I'm also quite certain I won't be able to think coherently about work once Lucy goes into labor.

Do yourself a favor here, men; think about this early and get *yourselves* ready. You don't want to be one of those guys who suddenly need to bolt, leaving a mountain of unhandled stuff in your wake, when you knew all along this was coming. Getting things ready in advance will prevent colleagues from hating you and bosses from thinking you're a terrible employee. Make a list of the most mundane, taken-for-granted things in your job that can't go undone for a couple weeks. This is, I am certain, going to be a lifesaver for me and maybe for you as well.

# 52

## *I'm Sorry, I Thought I Heard You Say …*

If I had to make a list of the top ten things I never thought I would hear Lucy say, the following anecdote involves a comment from her that would be number four (right behind, "Salma Hyek is at the door; she wants to know if we can have a three-way. You game?" and right ahead of, "Look, I know I shouldn't, but I just really, *really* like crack.")

On Saturday, while emptying the car of groceries, Lucy sneezed and then suddenly shouted, *"Damn it!"* When I inquired as to what the problem was, she said, "I just peed my pants a little bit."

The list of indignities women suffer in the name of bearing children got just that much longer. Other changes for Lucy in the past couple weeks included significant swelling in her hands and feet. As of a week or so ago, Lucy was no longer able to wear her wedding rings or many of her shoes. Lucy took to soaking her feet in ice water at every opportunity, but sadly, this did not help.

For those of you out there, if swelling in the extremities becomes a factor in your journey down this road, best to mention it to your GYNie. This could be a symptom of preeclampsia, a potentially dangerous condition for Mommy. If the swelling is coupled with high blood pressure, it's definitely something to be concerned about. In Lucy's case, the swelling is normal. Annoying, but normal.

At this point, our visits to the GYNie moved to weekly. The only addition to the previously documented routine was the doctor started doing a pelvic exam. The examinations for both weeks thirty-six and thirty-seven were unremarkable, and everything seemed to be going along swimmingly. At the end of the thirty-seven-week checkup, I asked the GYNie if she had any indications at this point as to how we are tracking in comparison to the ETA. The doctor replied that there are no indications the baby might be on her way imminently. Lucy was one-centimeter dilated, but this was actually normal, she told us, and given that the baby had not yet descended in the uterus, it was not an indication that Lucy was ready to go into labor. "However," she added, quickly crushing my rising certainty, "I could say that, and your water could break as you leave the office. There's just no way to know for sure." Excellent.

We also toured the maternity ward of the hospital during the thirty-seventh week. This was a very valuable exercise, and I decided I would recommend to anyone if their hospital provided these tours. They were able to answer a ton of questions for us regarding things we wouldn't want to worry about once the big moment was upon us. We certainly wouldn't want to have found ourselves trying to figure out where to park or check-in once labor had started.

Now, if we could just finish getting everything in order for the big moment. So far, we've been lucky that our daughter has not decided to come out early. We don't yet have Lucy's bag packed, and we don't yet have a car seat. (Lucy's uncle is getting the car seat for us as a gift; it just hasn't arrived yet.) I'd say we're likely about 90 percent of the way through preparations, but that last 10 percent is a laundry list of little crap that really needs to get done. If we have to tackle these under the duress of the moment, it could be a real problem. We're going to really have to power through the list this weekend. (The number of Fridays in a row we have been saying that now stands at six.)

For those of you going through this or about to go through this, here's another bit of advice in case you haven't picked up on it already: assume the end of week thirty-six is your due date. Have the bags packed by then, the route to the hospital memorized, call lists for family members ready, and as I suggested previously, details worked out at your job. I know this stuff seems pretty basic, but we're really coming to understand how critical it is. I have to admit that if the baby showed up today, it would be pretty challenging for us just getting out the door. That's not the way things should go when heading out to the hospital for this sort of event.

# 53

## *Zero to Sixty in Four Seconds Flat. Sixty to One Hundred in Five Hours*

The Saturday of week thirty-seven, Lucy and I went to a baptismal class in preparation for a later ceremony at the church where we had been married. We started the morning off with some tea and food and made our way to the church. The class itself was surprisingly interesting. Not that I was expecting a bad class or anything of that nature, but I was just a bit surprised it was as interesting as it was. This was due in large measure to the relaxed format and the relative lack of "preachiness." Afterward, we went about getting more of our preparations in order.

Our goal for the evening was to have our last date night before the baby arrived. We were going to have a nice dinner out and catch an 8:00 PM showing of *WALL-E*, which came out on Friday. At about 7:05 PM, we were preparing to leave for the movie (and I was finishing up the preceding section of this book) when I heard from the other room, "Uh, Bill … I'm not sure, but I think my water just broke."

My interest was raised. I responded with the most natural reply: "What do you mean, 'I *think*'?"

"Well, I needed to go to the bathroom anyway, so I'm not sure. It wasn't really a 'gush' like I expected, so I'm not sure," she answered.

Deciding it was likely a false alarm, I didn't get overly excited. I suggested we wait a bit and see if the possible water continued to flow or trickle or whatever it might do. After about twenty minutes, Lucy reported it was continuing to trickle and there had been one more somewhat considerable flow. To make it even more interesting, now there was a hint of blood.

The GYNie, as well as the instructor for the birthing class, had told us to call the doctor if we saw any blood at any point, so we called. Lucy reached the answering service, which was not surprising considering it was now nearing 7:30 PM on Saturday. Of course, as if the previous section of this book was a jinx, our lack of preparation was biting us in the ass. We went about the business of continuing to pack Lucy's hospital bag—thankfully we had a list to check off. Within ten minutes, the on-call doctor called back, and Lucy described the events of the past thirty minutes. The doctor told her there was a fifty-fifty chance her water had broken, and with the presentation of the blood, she wanted us to head in to the hospital right away instead of waiting for the contractions to start and then progress to a regular interval.

Lucy was pissed, and I was daunted. We had been told, after all, the first stage of labor can easily last upward of ten hours and we should be careful not to head in to the hospital too soon, or we risk sitting in an uncomfortable hospital room during the early stage of labor when it could be better spent in the comfort of our home. In our case, the contractions hadn't even started yet. "Damn it," she said. "I didn't want to get to the hospital this early! It's too soon. Plus, we're not ready. She can't come now."

We continued to pack and get ready to go, although Lucy was dawdling a bit, clearly unwilling to get to the hospital any sooner than necessary. In fact, she stopped for a moment so I could take a couple late-in-the-pregnancy pictures of her standing next to the crib, something that, like so many other things, we'd been planning on doing but had never gotten around to. (To my amusement, one of the pictures was taken at the moment of a more considerable "gush," so Lucy had a forced smile on her face, with her eyes saying, *"Take the picture, take the picture, take the picture!"*)

At about 7:35 PM, the first contraction came. I started my stopwatch. The second contraction came thirty minutes later. That was the moment all elements of predictability went out the window. The progression of contractions from there went as follows (Note that I had two jobs here: time the contractions and get Lucy to the hospital, so you can be pretty sure the below times are accurate):

- Time from first to second: thirty minutes—Duration: forty seconds
- Time from second to third: twenty minutes—Duration: forty seconds
- Time from third to fourth: fourteen minutes—Duration: forty-eight seconds
- Time from fourth to fifth: seven minutes—Duration: one minute
- Time from fifth to sixth: four minutes—Duration: one minute
- Time from sixth to seventh: three minutes—Duration: one minute

In one hour and fifteen minutes and a mere six total contractions, we had rocketed from "Eh, why rush, we have ten hours or so to get to the hospital" to "Holy crap, keep your legs together, Lucy!" In fact, the progression of the contractions was so fast, I was internally convinced it was false labor. Still, at around 8:40 PM (between the fourth and fifth contractions, in retrospect) we left for the hospital, and my speed increased with each contraction. By the sixth and beyond, Lucy was saying, "Don't speed, Bill!" Personally, I was a bit bummed; this was the one time in my life not a cop in the world would give me a ticket for speeding. (Okay, one would. About five months ago, I was pulled over by a CHP officer, who, for the purposes of this story, I will call Officer Jerkface, for going sixty-eight in a sixty-five in the left lane of the freeway. Jerk.) If we were lucky, we'd even get one of those cool police escorts we always see in the movies. What a letdown.

We arrived at the hospital at 9:00 PM and were in the room by 9:05 PM. The contractions, at this point, were coming regularly every three minutes and were becoming increasingly unpleasant for Lucy. I asked the nurse, Jennifer, if this was false labor or the real deal, and she said, "I'm pretty sure this is the real deal."

Lucy began getting undressed and into her gown, Jennifer began getting Lucy strapped into the various monitors, and I began the process of calling a few of the need-to-knows, which included Lucy's Aunt Patty. Aunt Patty lives in Denver but was planning on being present for the birth. I told her that it appeared she was going to miss the actual birth as the baby seemed determined to come that night but that it would be great if she could come in as soon as possible. I also texted my four closest friends all with the following responsible fatherly message: *DUDE!!! WE'RE HAVING OUR BABY TONIGHT!!!* (One of these friends, Bald-Eric, someone I've known since I was five, called me and started yelling, "We're going to be daddies!")

At that moment, Lucy was only three-centimeters dilated, but her labor was progressing so fast that Jennifer said the baby was definitely coming that night. When I inquired about the time frame, she told me the progression is typically 1 cm per hour, and Lucy needed to get to ten before we can really start the process of making things happen. So, in all likelihood, we had around seven to ten hours, but that was, of course, a guess.

By 9:30 PM, the contractions were growing in significance, yet Lucy was being a champ and not a single profanity was uttered.

The next sixty minutes were a blur. Too many phone calls to count from concerned and excited friends and relatives kept me running in and out of the room, Lucy's contractions were coming one after another, and Lucy's boss arrived—and thankfully brought me some dinner. Eventually, the contractions were so severe, Lucy decided there was no way she could do this without an epidural, so I asked Jennifer to arrange for it as soon as possible. One contraction, which Lucy came to call "the screamer," shot two-thirds of the way across the chart on the tape feeding continuously from the machine that was flashing and beeping.

Unfortunately for Lucy, the anesthesiologist was stuck in an emergency C-section and could not come in to provide the epidural as quickly as any of us, especially Lucy, would have liked. Finally, at 10:30 PM, she came in to provide the epidural, at which point, I excused myself so I could 1) call Aunt Patty back and let her know how quickly things were progressing and 2) avoid passing out when they stuck a large needle in my wife's spine. After the epidural, Jennifer checked to see how Lucy was progressing and was shocked to find her 8-cm dilated. In other words, in just under ninety minutes, Lucy's body had progressed five hours worth. It was at this point Jennifer said to me, "Your daughter could be born in the next hour or two."

It was at that point I began my freak out.

Three-and-a-half hours into a process everyone told me could take twenty or more, we seemed to be nearly at the finish line. I couldn't understand how this was, but there was nothing I could do but keep my head about me and see what, if anything, I could do for Lucy. I went back into the room to find a much calmer Lucy, newly hopped-up on drugs from the midpoint of her back down. We chatted for a while and things were, mercifully, much more relaxed. At one point, I looked over at the tape being methodically emitted from the monitor and felt compelled to ask Lucy if she was feeling anything. "Nope, not a thing, why?" I reminded her of the screamer contraction for comparison's sake and told her she was currently experiencing one that was quite literally off the chart.

Up to this point was zero to sixty. Now begins the sixty to one hundred.

As can happen with epidurals, the process began to slow down considerably. The contractions, which Lucy could no longer feel but I could see on the tape constantly feeding from the monitor, began to slow in frequency and level off in intensity. Jennifer, nurse extraordinaire, had started having Lucy push with contractions at around 12:00 AM, not with the intent to try and deliver, but to get the baby moved into position and assess how close we really were. This stopped around 1:30 AM as the contractions ceased altogether. For the next ninety minutes, little happened. At 2:00 AM, Aunt Patty called to see how things were going, as she was unable to sleep. She had secured a 9:00 AM flight to the Bay Area and was anxious for news. We had no news to give, but the call enabled her and Lucy to talk for the first time during the entire process, which was just great for both of them. My friend, Big Mike, also called me to demand an update. He and his fiancée were less than pleased with me as I had neglected giving them status updates after my initial text and they were now both too excited to sleep.

At 3:00 AM, Jennifer stated they wanted to induce labor to get the process started again. The first attempt to induce did not restart the process, but the second, at 3:30 AM, resulted in immediate and strong contractions. At 3:50 AM, after more pushing to get the baby ready, another nurse, Linda, decided Lucy was ready to deliver and called the GYNie. The doctor came in at 4:07 AM, and, after just two real pushes, our daughter, Aleesia, was born at 4:10 AM on Sunday, June 29. She came in at a respectable eighteen inches long and an even six pounds. She was set on Lucy's stomach immediately, and the two began staring at each other, finally meeting on the outside.

# 54

## *The Aftermath and the Name*

Nine hours and five minutes from the moment Lucy first suspected her water had broken, we had our daughter. All in all, despite how long it took me to describe it here, it was a relatively short and smooth process (says the one involved who didn't deliver a baby). Nine hours from start to finish, and the delivery itself was complication-free and only took two pushes. After the first push, I told Lucy I could see the top of the head and one of our daughter's ears. After the second, I could see the rest of the head and neck. In what seemed like just a moment, I saw our daughter in the doctor's hands. In fact, the delivery was so smooth, Lucy didn't immediately realize Aleesia had been born. This was something that was, undoubtedly, a side effect of the epidural. After the second push, I could see Lucy warming up for another before I told her our daughter was here and she didn't need to push any more. She looked at me with a puzzled expression and asked, "Really?"

For any woman out there who suddenly hates my wife for the ease and quickness of the delivery, well, there's nothing I can do about it, so tough. Everyone's experience is different, and there's nothing I can offer up in the way of helpful nuggets except to say, epidurals rock. I hear so many people saying their primary reason for wanting to go without epidurals is that the baby and mother are not "drugged out" after delivery and don't lose their initial bonding time. After going through it, though—or rather, after watching Lucy go through it—I can say I don't understand this argument. I recall now Lucy being absolutely alert and coherent, and as long as she wasn't trying to get up and walk around, one would never have known she had any drugs in her system at all. She was so alert, as a matter of fact, that she wouldn't allow me to take the first picture of her holding Aleesia until after she had brushed her hair. I also recall Aleesia appeared completely alert. Granted, I didn't make her take a drug test or anything, but I really didn't get the feeling she was affected in any meaningful way. So while I was only an interested observer in this process, that argument seems a nonissue to me. I've heard others say they don't want epidurals because they believe them to be unnecessary and dangerous, given that a large needle is being stuck into their spine. There's nothing I can say about that, so if that's your feeling on it, you get no argument from me.

In the end, I was in the delivery room for the birth and was glad of it. It was not the gore-fest I had been so concerned about, although you better believe I didn't investigate too closely the goings on down south. (The smell, however, was not pleasant.) Fortunately, the word "crowning" was never used during the process, but obviously it would've been an accurate description of at least a period of the events. I happened to catch a glimpse of some of the early crowning moments and it was, as I expected, unnerving. At least during the early points, it wasn't horror-film I'd expected to see but it was definitely not something for a greeting-card image. I think I handled it pretty well given I didn't pass out or throw up, however I wasn't rushing to see how the image evolved as things moved along. As the delivery progressed, my vantage point afforded me an opportunity to see the moment our daughter was free of her confines without having to witness whatever her expulsion had done to my wife's nether region.

Despite my making it through the delivery without vomiting and without injury to myself, I was still in no position to be doing anything as aggressive as cutting the umbilical cord. When the doctor asked, I declined, and the nurse came to my aid telling the doctor, "No, he doesn't need to cut it."

As if to prove my decision not to cut the cord was the correct one, the doctor had difficulty cutting it saying it was, "A really tough one."

Seeing mother and daughter for their very first moment together was truly special. After the nurse set her on Lucy's stomach, Lucy started talking to Aleesia, who seemed to instinctively realize this person was someone of significance and stopped crying. The two stared at each other for what seemed like several minutes.

I held my daughter for the first time at 4:16 AM. She was a mere six minutes old. I cannot imagine a more significant event ever happening in my life. She was swaddled and cleaned up by this point, and she seemed largely indifferent to my presence, but I was okay with that and stared at her for several minutes before handing her back to Lucy.

I left the hospital at 5:30 AM to let the dog out and try for an hour of sleep, after which I would go pick up Aunt Patty at the airport. By the time I returned with Lucy's aunt, my parents were in the room visiting Lucy and their thirteenth grandchild.

As for our daughter's name, this was a challenge right from the start. Given how long we had been trying to have a child, we had been thinking about names for some time before Lucy was actually pregnant. For some reason, we decided on a boy's name within minutes, but a name for a girl eluded us. Lucy had suggestions, all of which I hated. Name after name was suggested by her and vetoed by yours truly. Chloe? Nope. Isabella? Nope. Emma? Nope. We'd argue because, while I was a pro at vetoing names, I had none to offer up myself. I simply couldn't think of any.

The summer before Lucy got pregnant, I had a business trip that took me to Paris and Rome. Lucy came along with me, and the two of us took some extra time to do some sightseeing, especially in Rome. One day, while walking to the Pantheon, Lucy and I noticed a woodworking shop. The shop caught our eye with its full-sized Harley Davidson made entirely out of wood sitting outside. We were walking through, eyeing the marionettes and clocks, when we both noticed, adorning the back wall, name plates clearly designed for people to purchase for their children. We looked the wall over hoping a name would jump out at us. One did: Annalisa. We loved it. It was unique and interesting, it was Italian, and it was—at least in our opinion—very pretty. (And it didn't seem to fit any of the potential pitfall categories I mentioned earlier.) So we left Rome with a first name but no middle name.

Over the next few weeks, we discussed it more and more and decided "Annalisa" was a lot of name and maybe we could find a way to shorten it a bit. "Alisa" was nice, and for a while, we considered it, but it seemed to lack a little of the spark "Annalisa" had. Adding another *i* gave it a little more flair, and we decided that was it. At that point, all we needed to do was decide on the spelling. We settled on a more phonetic approach to prevent people from calling her "Alicia." So with roots in Rome plus a little poetic license, we have "Aleesia." (Pronounced a-LEE-see-ah. I'm hoping this pronunciation guide wasn't necessary, and you just read it that way; otherwise, we have goofed. Aleesia, do let us know what your teachers call you when they do roll-call on the first day of each school year.)

The middle name was my contribution, as I mentioned much earlier. From the time we returned from Rome with a first name in hand, the discussion turned to middle names. Neither of us could settle on one, each pooh-poohing the suggestions of the other. Then, months later, with the middle name still an open question, we found out Lucy and I were finally going to be parents. We were thrilled beyond description but extremely nervous waiting for confirmation of the pregnancy. We had seven days before the first doctor's visit to worry and sweat. For a week, all I could think of was how much I wanted everything to go well and how desperately we wanted to hear the doctor say everything looked as it should.

The day of that first doctor's visit was a long one. Leading up to the appointment, the clock seemed to tick backward, and all day long, all I could think was, *I hope everything is okay* or *I hope we really are going to have a baby.* As the day went on, I couldn't even manage this much, and the theme had worn down to be just plain, *I hope.* As I came back from lunch, I was listening to the most recent Rush album, *Snakes and Arrows,* with these thoughts swirling around my head when the eighth song on the CD started playing: a beautiful acoustic-guitar instrumental called, *Hope.* The song suddenly became a soundtrack for my day and the preceding week with all of my wishing for good news, not only from the doctor that day but also for the long road. Then, sitting in the car listening, I knew that was the name: Aleesia Hope.

Since then, the song has had new meaning for me, and in some ways, I wonder if that's the true meaning Alex Lifeson was aiming for when he wrote it. Not that he was thinking someone would name their kid Hope or that it had anything to do with a kid at all, but that this feeling of wonder and awe that is born from the hope for good things leaves you thinking that so much is possible if you can find a way to reach out and take it. This is what I remember hoping for when we found out we were going to have a baby, and it's what I hope Aleesia will feel as she grows up. I realize it's pretty difficult to glean all of this from an acoustic-guitar instrumental; however, the song seems to convey the feeling of looking for something more, that some expected *thing* is coming. It feels as though there's something on the horizon that, even if you don't know what it is yet, you know is there and will be great.

# 55

## *Last Bit of Advice*

On the subject of visitors after a baby arrives, not surprisingly, people have differing views, so this is something for you to really think about. Having someone there to help the mother during and after the birth, I can now say, can be a huge benefit if she's the right person. This is especially true if, like Aunt Patty, this is someone who has been through childbirth herself and can really relate to the couple.

If you are considering having a friend or relative stay with you to help during the time immediately after your baby arrives, be very careful about whom you enlist. You may have many volunteers, but think carefully about what will be on your plate after the baby arrives and how that may impact you. During the first few days or so with your new baby, there will be plenty of trips to stores for items you didn't realize you would need, the natural worries about pretty much everything your baby does or doesn't do, and the overall stress of just finding normalcy to your new routine not to mention cleaning up and getting yourselves and your house organized. Let's not forget the lady in your life is going to be more than a bit under the weather for a period of time as well.

Aunt Patty has been spectacular and invaluable, and we are blessed and thrilled to have her here. Of course, this is partly because we love her and she's so great but also because she gets what needs to be done during this time. She understands (and this is big) that the new mother may need some space from time to time. Apart from being there for support and overall help with Aleesia, Aunt Patty has helped clean and organize, which has been invaluable as neither of us have the mental wherewithal to clean and organize by ourselves.

What it boils down to is, if you are going to have someone stay with you to assist once your baby is born, make sure it's someone who's been through it, who has a level head, and who can help without taking over. Be sure it's someone you get along with and who will forgive how stressed you may become. It needs to be someone who can relate to you and who gets you. If you don't have anyone in your life that fits this tall order, you may be better off without a visitor for the first few weeks, even if you risk offending parents or in-laws by suggesting they hold off on the visits. Having the wrong person, even someone you love and are close to, can stress you and your spouse out and fracture relationships.

As for us, we are very fortunate to have so many relatives on Lucy's side who would fill this role admirably as would my sister or mother, and we would've been lucky to have any one of them helping us during this time. However, except for my mother, all of our relatives are in other states, and not everyone can suddenly leave town and stay with another couple for days or weeks on end even though they wish to. Aunt Patty simply happens to have been to be best positioned to come out here, and we are truly blessed that she is here.

As long as I'm on the subject, Aunt Patty, if you read this, thank you and we love you. We will never forget how much you have given us during this time, and we will never be able to repay you fully. Your help, support, kindness, and love are not only beyond what anyone could ever ask or hope for, they're exactly what we knew you and the entire family would always have for us. There really is no adequate way to describe just how much it has meant to us that you came and helped, and shared in this time with us, so I will simply say, from the bottom of my heart, *thank you.* Just your being here has been a welcomed and appreciated addition, but all that you've done for us while here is valued more than we can possibly tell you. (Note from later: Thank you, Uncle Mick, for loaning her to us. I was impressed and relieved when Aunt Patty told us later that the damage to the house was minimal. And, to Lucy's mom, Sharon, I trust you know we were definitely bummed it worked out such that you weren't able to be here during the birth, but we were so happy you made it out so soon afterwards. Of course, the logistics were pretty tough given we didn't know when Aleesia was going to arrive so it was just not going to be easy. We know how much you wanted to be here and we definitely wanted you here too. Certainly, it would've been wonderful if you could've been here when Aleesia arrived, but it was great you came out so soon after. Thank you! We love you!)

To our mothers, aunts, sisters, and cousins, we thank you for your eagerness and willingness to travel to be here and help. We thank you for the excitement you shared with us as we went through this entire process, and we know each of you would have been first in line to help if the circumstances had allowed it and we also know it would've been wonderful having any of you here to help. You guys are really just wonderful people and we are so lucky to have you all. We love you all.

# 56

## *Okay, One More Little Bit*

I'll briefly go back to the topic of getting yourself ready for the birth. As another part of that, it's a good idea to write a list of everyone you will need to call about your baby's arrival. Keep this checklist handy.

Obviously, this is good so you don't forget to call anyone, possibly offending them for eternity, but it's also helpful to check names off as you make your calls just so you remember whom you've already called. This may sound so easy you don't need a list, but don't forget you may be making these calls with little or no sleep.

In my case, I was running off about ninety minutes sleep in a thirty-hour span. When I called one of my very best friends, Mark, and said, "Well, my daughter's arrived!" he was confused as to why I was calling him because, of course, I had called earlier. (I still don't remember calling him the first time. And this is one of my closest friends! Of course, he may have been screwing with me; any friend of mine certainly has the potential to do so.) Just remember, you're going to have a lot on your mind and very little sleep to support it all. Give yourself as many tools at your disposal as possible.

# 57

## *Wrap Up*

It is 3:30 AM on Wednesday, July 2; my daughter's first night at home. I woke up to complete silence a short time ago, calmly, yet completely awake. The first thing that went through my mind was to wait and listen for some noise from our daughter to tell me she was still alive. Obligingly, a tiny "ack" was offered from her bassinet after a short while. At that point, however, my mind racing, there was no way I could go back to sleep. I decided, therefore, to put some final thoughts down before I risked losing them.

On her first night home, our daughter has slept five uninterrupted hours so far. While excellent, the first two hours of that were wasted on my wife's part and mine, as we were still awake. Depending on how the next few nights go, we may have to work out some complex process of keeping her awake until a more traditional time for us to go to bed.

In forty minutes, it will be exactly seventy-two hours since I became a father, and I am in considerable awe of the little being that, just a moment ago, kindly gave me a tiny little sound to reassure me that, at least for now, all is right. I find myself watching her intently throughout the days. As she sleeps, she is constantly running through a spectrum of facial expressions ranging from intense concentration to great happiness. (I can't imagine what a three-day-old baby dreams about, but it would be great to know.) When awake, she spends the time when she is content just looking around the room—sometimes doing so with her mouth gaping open, giving the impression that she's awestruck by whatever she is looking at. I have been told a baby's field of vision is limited to just a foot or so when they're this young, so I suspect, if that's the case, she's seeing shapes and lights flying by and it's enthralling to her. When she is not content, she is, predictably, screaming until we can find out what she needs in order to become content.

As I look back over the past eight-and-a-half months, I am struck by the seeming ease and casualness with which we have crossed the line from couple to parents. Looking back at the relative smoothness so far, I begin to wonder if we understand the road that lies ahead. After all, there's no chance life with our daughter will be so problem free (I am knocking on wood with each sentence I type), yet she came into the world with an ease that could give us a false sense of security that we're actually ready for what is in store.

I will say there is no doubt we are unprepared for what hit us last weekend when we became parents—unprepared both tactically and emotionally. I'm beginning to suspect that's the point, though, as this is a life-changing experience that nobody can ever really prepare for. To try and prepare outside the obvious ways to do so—getting rooms ready, securing things that one will need to take care of the coming child, and so on—may be close to a waste of time and may fool the intense planner into an unwarranted calmness or the nonplanner into a complete meltdown. I remember the couple in our birthing class taking those intensely detailed notes for their big event, and I wonder what their experience will be like. Will they be able to deal with the bumps that are thrown their way in such an unplannable series of events? Will it throw them for a loop, or will they recover as gracefully as they're planning to?

As I said, the relative ease with which our daughter came into this world—even the pregnancy, in hindsight—belies the significance of the event itself. Possibly the smoothness of the road to this point is a reflection of my and Lucy's change in attitude toward the unknown. Up until now, being even somewhat unprepared for anything would have caused Lucy anxiety to the point of insomnia. It would have caused me to take an approach of "Don't worry about it. Let's see what happens and react accordingly," while constantly checking peripherally to see if everything is okay. I see now that neither of these approaches is going to work alone. Some twisted hybrid of the two is needed, and now, a mere seventy-two hours from the moment when little Aleesia Hope was first set on Lucy's stomach, I'm okay with the need for a new mindset about the unknowable road ahead of me. For the first time since I met my wife, her response to small yet significant details (such as those involved with driving our daughter home for the first time) has been a casual shrug and, "Eh, do what you want to do." As for me, I'm mired in the minutia of how to change a diaper correctly and quickly check if our baby is too hot or too cold. What happened to us?

I will have to look back occasionally to see how exactly my outlook evolves (as it most certainly will) as new input is incorporated and see how long new changes stay in place before they, too, are modified. Also, it will be interesting to see how these changes affect how we think about things that seemingly have nothing to do with our child. No matter what we do on this road, no matter what we try to do differently or better, we and all things around us will obviously be impacted, and these things can never be erased. After all, once a change is in place, things can never be as they were before, even if the circumstances are reverted. We can only move forward on the timeline that now involves our daughter and see how things keep moving. As a great song writer, Neil Peart, wrote, "Changes aren't permanent, but change is."

Whatever the road looks like ahead of us and whatever it looked like getting up to this point, I can now honestly look back at the hundreds of people who asked me if we're ready and say for the record, "No, we are not ready." And, to be honest, I'm good with it that way.

# EPILOGUE

# The First Months

# 58

## *Two-Month Check-in*

It was not my intention to add an epilogue to my little story, but as today was August 29, our little girl's two-month-iversary, I found myself reflecting on the past two months, so I decided to add a bit on what's transpired. Of course, there has been tremendous change in Lucy and myself and our day-to-day operations, but seeing the change in our attitudes and activities hasn't been nearly as significant as seeing the physical changes in Aleesia.

Weighing in at an even six pounds at birth, our daughter was a tad on the diminutive side. She was small to the point where, when I held her, I could lay her in my hands, her back from butt to shoulders supported almost entirely in my left hand and her head in my right hand. The skin on her legs seemed too big for her as though she was wearing a baby suit meant for a slightly older baby. Because she was smaller than we had been expecting and preparing for, when we brought her home, we had only one outfit that was small enough to really fit her and only about six others that would suffice despite being large. We had no appropriately sized sleep wear and no diapers that would fit her beyond those we'd taken with us from the hospital. Therefore, my first day with mother and baby at home was spent making eight individual shopping trips to secure additional things we needed for a smaller baby. Day two required only six trips. Part of the reason for so many trips was discovering additional things we needed, and part was not finding a store that carried the size diapers we needed. (In retrospect, I laugh at how I naively thought I would be able to "get a little work in" the first week we had Aleesia at home. I figured she would spend most of her time sleeping and so would Mother, and I could just get some things done here and there. What an idiot.)

At the end of the first month, I suddenly became aware she fit her skin much better and was shocked to find her head was much more sizeable in my right hand. Where before it was around the size of a baseball, after a month, it was just under the size of a softball. Her first outfit had been outgrown, and we were up a size in diapers. Obviously, it wasn't surprising how quickly a newborn baby grows, but it was pretty amazing to witness it firsthand. After all, when we were growing up, we saw our friends growing quickly, but because we were doing so at the same time, we tended not to notice the more remarkable changes. At Aleesia's one-month check in, she had gained two pounds and two inches in length—a whopping one-third bodyweight increase!

# 59

## *A Tale of Two Families*

After that first week when Aunt Patty was here, Lucy's mother and father also came out for a visit, as did my sister and a couple friends of mine. The difference in the reactions of our two families to Aleesia was remarkable and a little amusing. As I mentioned previously, for my parents, Aleesia was the thirteenth grandchild, so their somewhat more relaxed response was understandable. Not that they were anything other than totally thrilled—it is just that the squealing and awe of the grandparents became slightly muted once the grandparents reached a baker's dozen. For Lucy's family, on the other hand, Aleesia was the first in the next generation. This vaulted Aleesia to near celebrity status immediately. It was quite endearing to see the intense love, curiosity, and fascination her parents had for Aleesia. Her mother could not stop touching Aleesia's feet and hands and kissing her forehead. Lucy's father would stare at Aleesia with nothing short of wonder and could not stop randomly saying, "Man, she's just beautiful." (He received no argument from me.)

On my side, however, my sister already dubbed herself Favorite Aunt and was prepared to battle to the death to defend the title should any challengers arise in an attempt to take it.

# 60

## *The Ever Present Volumes of Poo*

While I realize in the spectrum of how vile feces can truly be, the samples provided by a two- to three-month-old baby are on the tamer side of the scale (probably just barely grosser than squirrel crap, although, I will admit I am no expert on squirrel crap), it's still poo, and it just isn't on my top-ten list of things I am stoked to get my hands dirty with. Fact is, in a testament to nature's ability to ease humans into unpleasantries in the interest of propelling the human race forward, the general grossness of poo seems to ratchet up as the baby ages, or more specifically, as the baby's diet changes. We're still at the early stages of the ramp up, so the smell isn't yet as horrible as it will no doubt be, but there's no shaking the fact it is poo. Untaping the diaper straps always comes with a sense of dread for what lies beneath.

This being said, I have managed to do fairly well in handling the cleanups so far. I have been told by others going through this that one gets used to dealing with a baby's messes pretty quickly, and, it would seem, this is not far from the truth. I'm reminding myself that her poo is not yet at its most disgusting, but I'm still taking credit for doing the changes without complaints or vomiting or even any gagging or dry-heaving, and I have yet to run to the army-supply store to pick up a gas mask or secure a bandana around my face in Western bank-robber style.

Lucy, on the other hand, has hit some potholes along the feces removal highway. First among them is our daughter's tendency to evacuate her feces at incredible velocities. This would not be nearly as annoying were it not for the fact that she tends to wait to deploy her most forceful fecal discharges until those precious few moments where

Lucy is changing her and Aleesia is briefly without a diaper. There's the added condition of these deployments being more a shotgun type disbursement than a stream or steady flow.

One night, Lucy was changing Aleesia on the couch downstairs at some ridiculous hour when, because it seemed like a good idea to her at the time, Aleesia decided to add a last-second deposit to what was already in the diaper. Once again, the rate at which Aleesia did so was, as described by Lucy, amazing. And, of course, seizing on the least opportune moment, the evacuation occurred while diapers were in transit. The deployment resulted in feces in a fanned-out disbursement several feet from the evacuation portal. Like an army sergeant jumping on a grenade to save his platoon, Lucy sacrificed herself, and 95 percent of the matter landed on her, sparing our upholstery almost entirely. Way to go, Lucy! Way to take one for the team! (Moral of this story: always place the new diaper opened up under the baby's butt before you untape the old, soiled one. You can use the old diaper like a squeegee to scrape down some of the poo now smeared across your baby's butt, and you can also stow the used wipes in it before pulling it out and taping it up for disposal. Then, if the child poos or pees while you're working, you've got a receptacle for it already in place with a handy flap—the front of the diaper—you can flip up to cover the flow. When the soiled diaper is removed, you've already got the new one underneath in case new deposits are added right away. There is just one more thing to look out for: for some reason, Aleesia seems to like sticking her foot in the poo in the old diaper until we can remove it. Be on the lookout for that.)

Of course, eventually it was my turn to take one for the team. This morning, a Sunday, Aleesia was placed next to me on the bed while I slept so Lucy could attend to nonbaby items. After a while Aleesia began fussing, so I picked her up and sat her on my stomach in a seated position, supporting her upright as I lay there. This mollified her for a short time, but then she began fussing again. It was at this moment I noticed a considerable smell emanating from my daughter's bottom region. Being a pro at the infant diaper changing now, I matter-of-factly set about changing her. Placing her on the changing mat, I noticed my hand was damp. Not just damp—there was "matter" on my hand. Suddenly, I noticed my shirt and shorts where similarly affected. Crossing myself and saying a silent prayer, I undid her diaper to find a volume of feces that suggested Aleesia was flushing her system like an old radiator. There was so much matter that, had it been a deposit of mine, I would've wanted a nap after. She's quite the overachiever, my kid.

As a side note, my friend Derek suggested the title of this section after pulling it from an e-mail I sent him, discussing Aleesia. I mention this for no other reason but to give him credit and to demonstrate that the style of this book really is pretty much how I talk and write all the time.

# 61

## *Okay, Enough of That*

Back to non poo-related subjects. Month two brought about an amazing change in Aleesia: she gained a fifth condition. Up to that point, her only conditions had been

1.  Asleep

2.  Eating

3.  Screaming

4.  Mollified (This was typically a coveted interim phase bridging the gap between any two of the first three conditions and could only be achieved when she was being carried by Lucy.)

At month two, her new condition to add to the list was: content.

In the mornings while we're getting ready for work, Aleesia recently began watching me or Lucy intently or simply looking around the room, kicking her legs about and making cooing sounds. This new condition also brought with it something amazing that started causing me to be late to work nearly every day: purposeful smiles. (Also known as smiles that are not a result of gas, which cause a variety of facial contortions.)

Her smiles have proven absolutely amazing. They would range from small grins with an accompanying growling sound all the way to what I named a "full-body smile." These were such significant smiles, they caused Aleesia to pull her arms and legs in suddenly as though the force of the smile requires the additional strength. These would typically be accompanied by a long piercing *e* sound.

Along with her *e* sound, Aleesia seemed to be finding her vocal cords more and more. Her cooing ratcheted up considerably, and she started making chatty noises nearly constantly when in a non-screaming condition. She seemed to surprise herself occasionally by emitting some sound she was unaware she had the ability to produce; she then got an excited look on her face and set about making that sound repeatedly until she had it down and could call it up whenever needed.

At her two-month check up, Aleesia weighed in at about ten-and-a-half pounds. In other words, she came within one-and-a-half pounds of doubling her weight in sixty days. The doctor had told us he wanted to see a sixty-ounce gain, and Aleesia, being an overachiever as I said earlier, put on seventy-two ounces.

The change in Lucy has been quite noticeable as well. When we first brought Aleesia home, Lucy was nervous about walking with her for fear of tripping and dropping her or even changing her for fear of hurting her. Lucy was also constantly checking Aleesia's temperature (not yet in the unpleasant way Aleesia will come to hate later). In fact, Aleesia's first ever bath outside the hospital was administered by myself as Lucy was far too nervous about dropping Aleesia to give the bath herself. Therefore, I took the reins and her first little sponge bath was done. Of course, Aleesia hated it and screamed the entire time, while Lucy took some wonderful pictures that will eventually be shown to a perspective boyfriend. Also, while I was giving the bath, she peed on me to demonstrate her displeasure with the proceedings. (Aleesia, not Lucy.) That was the second time in my daughter's first five days outside the womb that she peed on me. The first time was at the doctor's office when I took her diaper off for her weigh-in.

Since that first week, Lucy has really settled in. Nothing really seems to freak her out any more, although—and I am again knocking on wood when I type this—we haven't yet had any illnesses or accidents to really test our metal. I'm sure, when those do come, they will be completely core-shattering, but the recovery will be quick and will leave us—and, theoretically, Aleesia—stronger for the experience. (Do I sound like I believe that? I'm working on it.)

On the topic of her screaming, my daughter has the unfortunate condition of being really funny when she's pissed off. She makes great faces when at her most displeased. This means, when she starts to really "pitch-a-fit" (or simply "pitch" for short), there are usually a couple minutes where, instead of my finding a way to pacify her, I grab the camera to snap a couple pictures of her. I don't think this makes me a terrible person, given that she screams out of want now more than any possible pain. (It's only later, when I'm showing all these pictures to perspective boyfriends, that I'll be a terrible person. I have no issue with this.)

Speaking of my relationship with my daughter, I'm 100 percent smitten by her. My office is full of pictures of her and my screensaver has been replaced by a montage of additional pictures (an equal allotment of ones where she's content, sleeping, smiling, and pitching). I race home every night now just so I can quickly change my clothes (important, given her battle tactics), pick up Aleesia, and just walk around staring at her when she'll let me. As I walk with her, her face becomes alive with curiosity about the scenery flashing by her. She's amazed by lights in the ceiling and tracks them as I turn while walking with her.

Aleesia, however, is somewhat less enamored with her father. I anticipate this will change in time (and am fully prepared to buy her affection if it is necessary to resort to such undermining actions), but it's more than a touch frustrating at this moment. Most of the time, I can pick her up at her most content, and within three minutes, she'll be screaming. I will employ all means of pacifying and distraction at my disposal, some of which will work for a time, but if she gets into full pitch, the only thing that will calm the storm is Lucy. As if to twist the knife even more, all Lucy has to do to calm an Aleesia in full pitch is pick her up. Very frustrating.

I am not naïve and realize there is a very understandable reason for this relationship between Aleesia and Lucy. After all, for the last several months in the womb, Aleesia was calmed by Lucy's voice and heartbeat, and once outside the womb, Aleesia was calmed by Lucy's smell, breath, and voice anytime she was feeding. It's only natural Aleesia would find Lucy a soothing port in a storm. I'm just longing for the day she starts leaning toward being "daddy's little girl" and we start to really form that bond. In case it takes too long, however, I've already started pony shopping.

As for the actual crying and screaming, Aleesia is pretty determined. If the torrent of screams goes unaddressed, Aleesia will start coughing and gagging from the effort. Lucy and I have become so desperate to keep Aleesia in the content phase that, when holding her, we have started singing tunes sporadically, walking in an overly bouncy way, swinging her wildly, and making ridiculously exaggerated faces and smiles. Our primary purpose in life, it would seem, is now simply to find a way to distract and mollify our baby for as long as possible. We are, effectively, rodeo clowns but without the make-up and who have to meticulously clean up the crap instead of avoiding stepping in it while running for our lives.

Recently, I discovered that Aleesia can be quieted to the point of falling asleep if I hold her and just walk around our downstairs for long periods. The scenery and lights passing by catch her interest and soothe her. Eventually, she falls asleep. Since then, during those times when she cannot be pacified by any traditional means (formula, pacifier, boob), I pick her up and walk large circles through the kitchen, into the dining room, around the living room, and back to the kitchen. Last week, I made one hundred ten laps along this course. Afterward, I measured one lap and, multiplying by one hundred ten, found the distance was in excess of a mile. Not only did the baby become totally pacified for a brief time, I also burned a few calories. Yet another win/win.

In an effort to help her linguistic development start off on the right foot, we are trying not to speak baby-talk to her, but our tones and inflections are impacted nonetheless. I often think Aleesia's impression of us has to be very odd. Even though she cannot yet understand what we're saying, she must think we're all excited to the point of ridiculousness at every minor detail. Also we're caught in some twisted musical that never ends for all the singing (but whose songs are really stupid and only last around ninety seconds). These songs are usually something like, "Who needs a diaper changed? *You do!* Who needs a diaper changed? *You do!*" I fear this way of dealing with her may begin to impact my everyday work. I can see now having a conversation with the senior vice president of my division; when he asks me why a customer is upset and complaining, I may just respond absentmindedly with, "Maybe he's poopy."

# 62

## Month Three and Stuff

At three months, Aleesia's growth has continued undaunted. She is, of course, even bigger now, coming in at around thirteen pounds. Additional outfits have been retired, and additional sleepwear has been procured to accommodate her new size. Also, a sixth condition has been added to her repertoire: amused.

This sixth condition typically shows up when Aleesia is watching Lucy and me getting ready for work in the morning. She watches us intently and randomly smiles, screeches happily, and blows spit bubbles. She's also fascinated with mirrors now. My closet door is mirrored and is right across from my vanity, so Aleesia switches between watching me "live" and watching me in the mirror. Back and forth she turns her head, I'm certain, in an effort to figure out which of the two daddies is the real one.

We also heard—and recorded on video for good measure—Aleesia's first ever true laugh. (Well, first ever that we're aware of. It's possible she's laughed when nobody was around to hear it. Sort of a baby version of the tree-falls-in-a-forest conundrum.) One evening last week, I was playing with Aleesia in front of a mirror. There I was, happily dancing her around and touching her clenched fists to her counterpart in the mirror while humming a tune for her, when suddenly she broke out in true laughter. I was blown away. It was, quite honestly, the very coolest thing I'd ever heard. Since that event, we regularly give her a bit of mirror time. I'm hoping this doesn't mean she's going to be intensely self-centered as an adult. There are just so many ways to screw up a child, I'd hate to do it unknowingly simply for her and my amusement.

Note from later:

I read that all babies tend to enjoy mirror time quite a bit. This is why toy companies are so often putting little mirrors on baby toys, strollers, and so on. I'm sure there is some psychological or scientific reason for this, which I could find if I wanted to investigate a bit, but I prefer to think that all babies are just aware they are probably, at that moment, as cute as they'll ever be so they're just incredibly vain.

Aleesia has also been getting stronger by the day. Last night, while holding her up, she made clear and obvious efforts to stand. She wasn't successful, of course, but there was definite intent there. I held her up so that her toes touched my lap, and she extended her legs forcefully. For about two seconds, I let her support herself—I still held my hands around her chest in case she fell; I'm not a monster—before she bent her legs and started the process over. Yes, it's clear there's some manner of pro sports in her future. We just have to settle on one. Or two.

# 63

## *Some Thoughts on Vaccinations*

Lucy and I have done a lot of researching and asking around on the topic of vaccinations, regarding both overall concerns and the possible link to autism. I will not be one in the throngs of people who will happily tell you what you should or shouldn't do. This is far too sensitive and personal a topic for me or anyone to tell you what to do. I will say, however, you should do your own research and ask around on this subject before you make any decisions. When it pertains to your baby, you should never listen to any single source without questioning the logic nor blindly follow the example of anyone else. Take as many differing opinions and facts in as you can before you decide what to do.

For us, deciding what to do about vaccinations was proving daunting. Living in the Bay Area gave us access to plenty of good and bad information and plenty of people who couldn't wait to tell us what to do or think or be worried about. In the end, we agreed vaccinations were a good idea, but we decided to temper Aleesia's with some prudence. Vaccinations followed a schedule—which any pediatrician will give you a copy of—but these schedules were really more guidelines than hard and fast rules. So we decided we needed a doctor whom we could ask more questions of and who would allow us to enter into the decision making. The most important thing for us was finding a doctor that was not a live-and-die-by-the-schedule type. Some advice for you: if your doctor has no flexibility whatsoever on the vaccination schedule and flexibility is important to you, then you shouldn't have flexibility with the doctor; find yourself a new one. Remember, in the end, you—not your doctor—are responsible for your baby.

We decided to space the schedule out a little more than was recommended. Many of these shot appointments are three to four vaccinations in one sitting. We felt that was a lot to handle and, if it didn't lessen the effectiveness of the vaccinations to spread them out, we thought that was probably better. Our doctor said this wasn't going to be a problem for most of the shots, but a few needed to be done in concert with one another or within a certain amount of time of the previous one. No problem for us; we extended what was safe to put on hold, and all was well.

The main one folks worry about is known as Measles/Mumps/Rubella (or MMR). This is the one that people who feel there is a link between vaccinations and autism believe is the likely culprit. I'll give a very brief description of the concern and the logic behind it as I have read it, but you'll want to do more research on this yourself: The concern relates to the mercury-based preservative added to the vaccination when the three individual vaccinations are combined. Also, some people believe the simple combination of the three is, in and of itself, an issue (that it seems a lot to give a toddler at once). According to the schedule, these shots are given at around fifteen to eighteen months of age. Many parents who, soon after, see the first signs of autism naturally feel that the shot caused the autism. The rebuttal from the medical society is these children would have had autism anyway and that the timing when it's first noticed is coincidental, as most children won't show any symptoms of autism until around eighteen to twenty-four months.

We will not take sides on the issue as there is no conclusive evidence available one way or the other. (Note, by the way, that according to our doctor, the preservative that is at the center of the controversy is no longer used.) However, we will err on the side of caution. When the time comes, our pediatrician will give each of the components of the MMR vaccinations individually and over successive visits. (Not all pediatricians will do this. Ask yours.) We will also wait a little longer to give Aleesia these shots to be more confident in her development when she gets them. Pediatricians are fine with giving the shots as late as twenty-four months, and by then, we should have a much better indication of Aleesia's development in relation to possible autism. This approach is potentially going to be an issue with daycare, however, as some insist on full vaccinations before admitting a child. This will be something to look into when the time comes, but we feel it's definitely the smaller issue of the two.

# 64

## *Months Four and Five ...*
## *Let the Drooling Begin*

Things really started to pick up around here. Since about halfway through month two, I found Aleesia was growing more and more comfortable with me. By the end of the month, I could hold her without her screaming, provided she wasn't already screaming at the time I picked her up. Over the following weeks, she began to respond when I came in the room and, in the mornings, would also flash a little smile at me during her morning routine of screeching happily and sucking on her toes. (She sucks on her toes a lot. Sometimes, both her right and left big toes at the same time. I don't know if she'll always have the flexibility required to suck on her toes, but I'm hoping she doesn't always have the interest or motivation to continue to do so.)

Over the past couple weeks, our relationship really turned a corner. Suddenly, when I came home from work, she started perking up when she heard me, letting out a loud happy screech, and giving me one of her gigantic smiles before burying her face into the chest of whoever was holding her at the moment. These interactions were typically the brightest moment in my day by a healthy amount.

Also lately, while sitting at the dinner table, she started just staring at me while Lucy was holding her. When I acknowledged her and give her a smile, she would reciprocate with another squeal and smile and then bury her face in Lucy's chest. The routine would then start all over again.

Perhaps most amazing of all, I even began having some success in mollifying Aleesia if she was fussing, crying, or screaming, provided

Lucy was not in the room. (I'm okay with being a second choice here.) This was proving a really helpful change because it meant I could help reduce the internal noise levels of our house without Lucy having to stop whatever she was doing.

Last weekend, however, Lucy and I went to a movie with some friends while my niece, Nik, watched Aleesia for us. When we arrived home and raised the garage door, we could see my niece taking Aleesia out of the stroller. No sooner had Lucy said, "Oh, how nice, they went out for a walk," did we hear Aleesia screaming with a fervor we had never before witnessed. I was surprised my car windows weren't being blown out. There was no question that, despite my newfound bonding with my daughter, I was going to have no success in quieting this super pitch-a-fit. Lucy got out and picked Aleesia up. The screaming quickly abated, but Aleesia spent an hour giving us the most pitiful look she could muster, staring at us with classic puppy-dog eyes, and, as if to make certain we were feeling sufficiently guilty, randomly doing that after-cry stuttering inhale that only kids can do. It was brutal. Lucy didn't put her down for hours, I immediately ordered a pony, and we both agreed we were not going out on a date-night again until Aleesia was at least thirteen.

Also, Aleesia began drooling profoundly at this point. If left to her own devices (meaning neither Lucy nor I are there to wipe her lip and chin and neck and hands), she would soon have enough drool on her onesie to look as though she was drenched in sweat after completing a marathon. Lucy was convinced this meant Aleesia's teeth were coming in. (Excessive drooling is one sign teeth are on their way.) Of course, had Lucy not been saying this daily for the past two months, I might have given somewhat greater weight to the possibility that teeth are actually causing the drooling. At the moment, however, I was just chalking it up to the fact our baby was still a baby, and babies tended to be more prone to drooling than adults. Also, I would occasionally run my finger along Aleesia's gum line and look for visible evidence teeth are coming in. To date: none.

As if to complement the drooling, my niece recently taught Aleesia to blow raspberries. It was absolutely adorable, no question. The only downside was that it magnified the drooling to new levels. When we would place Aleesia down in her crib or place her in another baby-centric area, she would lie there and just buzz away. If we left her there long enough, she would literally have a pool of drool on her throat and on whatever she was lying on at the time. It's adorable, really. She has also taken to jamming her entire fist into her mouth, getting it good and slimy with drool, then wiping it on us. She really is my kid, no question about it.

Also, at four months, Aleesia has learned to roll over front to back and back to front. Now if left on her play mat and not closely monitored, she'll roll right out of the room.

Month five found Aleesia's continued growth in many areas. She was still very chatty in the morning, but at that point, when she woke up, instead of immediately seeking attention, she would lie there and look around, making noises. I found myself watching her do this, thinking what a, well, almost "grown up" thing to do. It was really something.

On the first Sunday after her five-month mark, I placed Aleesia in a sitting position on our bed and let her go to see what she would do. I did this fairly regularly, and, every time, the only change in what she did next was which direction she'd fall over. Typically, she'd slowly fall forward as though she was being deflated, so that, if I didn't stop her, she'd be lying completely flat on her stomach with her legs outstretched alongside her torso. (This never looked very comfortable but she didn't seem to mind. She's definitely more flexible now than I suspect she will be later.) When she'd fall sideways or backwards, it would be with a rather amusing flop.

This time, however, she stayed upright. She placed her arms at her sides to stabilize herself and just sat there, looking around as though this was the most normal thing in the world. I was amazed and called Lucy up, and we both stared at Aleesia for a few minutes until she plopped over backward, out of what appeared to be nothing more than boredom of sitting up.

I sat her up and she stayed up again. This time, Lucy popped open the camcorder, and we captured about four minutes of what I'm sure would be inane and boring footage to anyone else. We were having a great time, though, and of course that's all that matters. After several minutes of sitting up, when it became abundantly clear Aleesia could now maintain a sitting posture when she wanted to, I very gently pushed her over backward to see if she could right herself. (Actually, it was because I thought it would be funny. I was right.) Like a wax sculpture of herself, she fell over backward in the exact position she had been sitting in and stayed that way for a little while. I was so pleased children are there as much for our amusement as anything else.

# 65

## *Stuff Everyone Will Say You Need, Except Me*

During the time Lucy and I were preparing for Aleesia's arrival, and for a time after she arrived, we encountered a steady stream of items we allegedly needed for Aleesia. These suggestions came from people volunteering their own experiences or from lists in doctors' offices and elsewhere. Many of these things I found were, at least for us, completely unhelpful and unnecessary.

I will add here a short list of some of the items that, either during the pregnancy or since, we have been told we need. A couple of these we find close to useless, but one or two items we won't do without. This is not an exhaustive list of course, and I'm not suggesting you should avoid or acquire any of these items. I'm just saying that not every item on every list out there will be pure gold. I am including just a couple items to get you started and to show you a more practical view of things folks will happily tell you not to try and live without. Look into the items here and on all of the larger lists you will come across, think about them practically and maybe hold back a little while you think about whether you actually will use some of the less obvious items. Below are my thoughts on these, your situation or your baby may mean different verdicts for these items and others.

- **Baby-wipe warmer**: The idea behind these is that the wipes used to clean a baby's behind are cold. A baby, presumably, is warm. When applied to a baby's bottom, the sudden cold from the wipes can be shocking and uncomfortable to them and may even cause them to pee. So warming the wipes up is helpful to keep things quiet as well as neat and tidy. For us, we find this device to be unnecessary for a couple reasons. First, we find the fluid on these wipes too harsh for Aleesia's skin, so we run them under warm water prior to using them. Second, unless you live in Alaska, it's winter, and you have no heating so you keep your child in a parka, it's unlikely the wipes are so cold compared to the temperature of your baby's butt as to cause a problem. Lately, we have started using the wipes without rinsing them first. We just hold them in our hand for a moment to warm them up if they do feel especially cold. Verdict: totally unnecessary.

- **Baby sleep positioner**: These are foam pieces that hold a baby on its side while sleeping so it cannot roll either forward or backward. One of the theories behind what causes SIDS is, when sleeping, babies might roll to their stomach and end up facedown on their blanket. They're not strong enough to push themselves back over and their lungs are not strong enough to breathe through the blanket, so they suffocate. We find Aleesia sleeps on her back and is not strong enough to roll over. In fact, she hates sleeping on her stomach. Also, she sleeps without any blankets at all and without a pillow. (Babies have a different idea of comfortable. They don't need pillows and they're not likely to need blankets. Back to my Alaska analogy: ideally, if they're wearing appropriate sleeping attire, they will keep plenty warm without blankets, provided the house has heating.) Verdict: unnecessary, at least for us. *Important*: Don't take my word for this. Like many other things, parents will have different opinions on these items and this is a sensitive topic since it relates to SIDS. Do research on this for yourself and see how your baby sleeps. If you decide these are not necessary for you, it doesn't make you a bad parent.

- **Crib bumper**: These are padded decorations that attach to the inside of a crib, surrounding the mattress. They are intended to add to the aesthetics of the crib and to prevent the baby from rolling against the crib posts and becoming trapped between the crib posts and the mattress. Interestingly, research I've read suggests that these may actually be dangerous if in the crib too early as they may trap a very small baby between the bumper and crib rail. When very young, a baby won't be strong enough to get out from the bumper if she becomes entangled. If you are worried about your baby getting trapped between the mattress and the crib rail, make sure you have the right size mattress for the crib. You will see, when they fit correctly into the crib, it would be pretty difficult for a baby to get trapped between them and the rail. Also, research I've found says that later, once the baby is able to pull herself into a standing position, these bumpers can be problematic. Babies bent on escaping their cribs will use them as a step to help them scale the sides of the crib and then fall over the side. You may think this unlikely, but let me tell you, Aleesia is already pulling herself up and over pillows and anything else in her path. Without a doubt, she would use the bumper if it were there. Given these factors, it appears there are only a couple months one can safely use the bumpers at all. In our case, we had the bumper in the crib purely as decoration before Aleesia was born and for a short time after we brought her home because she never rolled around, but then we eliminated it. As long as I'm on the subject, I really don't understand why babies are so intent on escape. Where do they want to go? Verdict: unnecessary and possibly dangerous if you believe the research. These come as part of most crib bedding sets, so you may end up with one regardless, but it's up to you whether you use it.

- **Mittens**: Unless you're taking your baby outside in the winter, these have nothing to do with keeping your baby's hands warm. For some reason, babies like to scratch at their faces, especially their eyes. They do it constantly. A baby's fingernails are sharp and will cut their faces and will definitely do damage to their eyes. Mittens are about the only way you can avoid that. We don't have any mittens, so I find a very acceptable workaround is to put a pair of her socks on her hands. This works wonders and has the added benefit of looking really funny. Verdict: must-haves. Socks will work, but if your lady balks at this silly-looking workaround, find yourself the mittens.

- **Diaper Genie (or similar)**: Babies poo. Babies poo a lot. Parents need a place to stow the soiled diapers until such time

178

as they're finally disposed of outside the house, and it should be a place that is designed for such a purpose. Any guest to the house will appreciate it. It needs to be something that will address the problem of the odor and make it convenient to remove and dispose of the diapers once there are a sufficient number of them. The kitchen or bedroom trash will simply not suffice here. You certainly don't have to use the same brand we did, but definitely invest in one of these handy items, whichever brand you decide on. It will be the difference between walking into your house eager to see the baby or walking in and gagging. Verdict: close to a must-have.

Here also are some other items you will need but not immediately. Do obtain these items but it's not a race. If you don't have them before you bring your baby home, you're not a bad parent and the walls won't come falling down around you. You have at least a couple months before your baby is even the least bit mobile.

- Playpen
- High chair
- Baby-proofing gear:
    o Cabinet locks
    o Toilet seat latches
    o Safety gates
    o Outlet covers

# 66

## *I Guess I Should Try and Be Helpful*

Realizing I could go on ad infinitum about various things related to my daughter if I wanted, I figure I should wrap things up once and for all and try to impart a few things I've learned since becoming a dad and then call it a day.

One key thing new fathers need to come to realize as quickly as possible is that your baby doesn't hate you. (At least, not yet.) For me, the first couple months with Aleesia were very challenging because I was so desperate to bond with my baby that I wanted to hold her all the time, but she was only focused on continued mommy-bonding time. When I picked her up, she immediately looked around for her mommy as though I was just the transportation device to get her from the crib to the boob. If she was in anything other than a completely happy mood, my picking her up would result in screams and tears within moments. Sure, I could have carried her around while she was sleeping, but if she woke up while I was carrying her, she'd get this look on her face as though she'd been horribly betrayed while she slept and then start crying.

Men, you have to realize this is just the way it's going to be, and that's okay. As I said before, your baby's entire world has revolved around his mommy since the moment he first had any senses to tell him there was a world. Your baby's mommy is probably going to be the only thing that can calm him for a couple months. Fact. Now that you know this, come to terms with it and be okay with it. Somewhere in the two- to three-month range, your baby is likely to start appreciating the other common beings in its world (you, the dog, television, random pieces of torn paper), and these things will then not only mollify but also provide him some joy as well.

Without a doubt, the second-greatest moment in my life was the first time Aleesia smiled out of true and honest recognition of me. (Greatest moment number one: holding her just after she was born, and number three: getting married. I'm not worried about the rankings as Lucy's would look the same.) That smile made the two months leading up to it 100 percent worth it.

So hang in there, you'll be fine, and your baby will come to appreciate and love you. (Well, provided you're not an asshole.)

Given that you may not be able to bond with your baby in any of the big and obvious ways for now, try and find other ways to participate. If Mommy and baby are napping, heck, lie down with them. This is a wonderful way to get some of that bonding time in. If you're walking around with your baby, who falls asleep in your arms, sit down in a big comfy chair and let your baby sleep on you as long as he will. Whatever you can do to kick start that bonding time and get those really nice moments in is time well spent. (I realize this paragraph may make me sound like a bit of a puss, but these things really can keep you from getting discouraged, so I don't really care. I do think you'll find this type of stuff helpful.)

Also, find a way to contribute. Your baby-mommy is, naturally, going to be taking on a lot of activities that just can't be delegated. In my case, with my not being able to really calm Aleesia for the first two months or keep her happy if she was awake, I began to feel as though I wasn't a very big part of the equation. Contributing in small ways eventually helped me to become a bigger part of the balance, and that was definitely a good thing. Just holding Aleesia so Lucy could make dinner (or, heck, my making dinner—it's not like I can't cook) or doing diaper duty from time to time was a help to Lucy and really helped me get in daddy-mode more completely. Remember; you and your lady are both going to be shifting away from your previous lifestyles quite a bit, so it's best to work in some of these helpful habits now while you're at it.

A quick thought on a not fun topic: the screaming and how you deal with it. Look, they're babies. They're going to scream and cry because it's really the only means of communication at their disposal.

There's absolutely nothing to be done about it. It's illogical, and your baby will have no concept of fairness, awareness of your mood, or respect for the clock. All I can say about this is, the moment you feel your frustration level rising because you can't quiet a particularly nasty screaming session, put your baby down in the bassinette or crib, walk away, close the door behind you, and let her scream for a few minutes while you collect yourself. If you get angry or frustrated, even if you manage to control your temper, your baby will pick up on it, and it will be even more difficult to calm her down. And if you don't manage to control your temper, well, let's just say you can't lose your temper when holding your baby. I know this sounds so basic it shouldn't need to be said, but do not, ever, *ever* shake your baby. Not only is it a stupid thing to do, as it can't possibly quiet a screaming infant, but it's dangerous. It is much better to take a couple minutes to get yourself together while your baby screams and then try again. Don't risk any accidents to your baby because you just "have to" get that crying stopped at 4:00 AM.

Here are a few other quick points:

- Poo won't kill you. Again, I'm not a big fan, but it's not exactly deadly. And, as long as we're on the subject again …
- The poo gets everywhere. A baby's poo has no consideration for the capacity of the diaper it's going into, and it will happily seep or flow around the edges on a semiregular basis. At least once a week, Aleesia fills her diapers beyond capacity (an event we've come to call a "poop-out"), and it will creep or flow up her back and stomach and out the leg holes, tainting the clothes on the other side of the diaper. Don't be surprised when you have outfits soiled soon after you leave the house or even right after you put them on the baby. Carry extra outfits everywhere you go. In fact, carry several of them. This is because, unlike most adults, a baby can have more than one significant poop event in a very short span of time. A baby's poo also has pretty incredible staining abilities, and those outfits that have been the most affected are sometimes stained beyond saving. In truth, I'm not sure I'd want to put her back in an outfit I knew had been heavily soiled anyway. The mental image would just be too strong. So in the trash they occasionally have gone. If

you want to try and save these outfits, feel free, but we haven't yet had a great deal of luck on the worst offended, and, unlike adult clothes, they're just not that expensive. This is especially the case with the onesies. These things tend to come in packs of three or five for $12, so I don't lose too much sleep over it.

- You will get puked on, peed on, drooled on, and sneezed on. (And probably poo'ed on though, to date, I've been much luckier than Lucy in this department. Knock on wood!) Deal with it. It's like death and taxes—inevitable.

- Find small ways to make yourself helpful to your lady. Small things like doing the dishes, changing a diaper, or even something as simple as taking the baby off her hands for a few hours can really go a long way toward making her life easier, which definitely makes your life easier.

- Being a dad is awesome. Enjoy it. Enjoy the small things, and try to really take them in. Revel in the smiles, the cooing, and the minor milestones, such as the first time your baby rolls over or sits on her own. Stare absentmindedly at the pictures and annoy others with them. Don't listen to anyone who says you're being insufferable or who says you're turning into a pussy. Any overly testosterone-laden guys out there who give you crap for helping out with your baby instead of playing hoops or for just enjoying spending time with your baby is either devoid of children (so they have no idea what they're talking about), a liar, or an idiot. None of these people matter when it comes to you and your bond with your baby. For me, Aleesia's smiles are simply the most magical things I've ever seen, and I'm trying hard not to miss any of them. And, while nobody else has to understand, I sure as hell won't listen to anyone tell me I'm wrong.

So that's about it. I do hope that my experiences are helpful to anyone reading this who is either going down the road as you read or getting ready to go down the road. If not helpful, I hope they are at least mildly entertaining. Whatever your experiences will be, I hope that you are able to find some similar highs and lows. (The lows are important too.)

For me, getting to this point wasn't always easy or fun, but if it was the culmination of all these experiences that led me to where I am now, with my amazingly beautiful wife and breathtaking little baby in the next room as I finish this off, then I wouldn't trade any one moment for anything in the world. I hope you feel likewise during your travels. Whatever your road looks like, make sure to stop from time to time and take some pictures along the drive. Time goes by much quicker than it seems, and soon, you'll have only those to help look back and remember.

The next couple weeks will bring Aleesia's baptism and first Christmas—then in the coming months—her first Easter and birthday. I cannot wait to experience these and watch Aleesia and Lucy experience them, but at the same time, I'm already trying to be careful to not wish Aleesia grows up too quickly. The past five months have been a blur, and I can see how easy it would be to blink and miss something huge.

Back to my roller-coaster analogy from earlier: the ride has definitely taken off now, and it's more amazing than I had expected or could've hoped for. Again, I know we have yet to really be tested against difficulty in any meaningful way, but so far I'm having a terrific time and never expected to be as enamored by this little baby as much as I am. Not that I wasn't expecting to love her and be really into being a dad, but the magnitude isn't something you can really anticipate.

Oh, one last thing, back on the topic of how the guestroom/nursery was arranged. The reader will recall the aesthetic stalemate Lucy and I were in with respect to the spare room and where the bed and crib should be placed. (I wanted it to make sense; Lucy wanted it to look like it did in her mind, regardless of what the laws of physics allow.) Well, when Lucy's Aunt Patty was here immediately after Aleesia was born, she was staying in that room. She took one look at how it was set up, the bed still sideways along the wall and the crib in front of it, and said, "Uh, wow. This is—uh, interesting." Just one little innocuous comment to Lucy later, and the room was oriented exactly as I had suggested originally which had been so quickly dismissed. I've not yet actually said, "Uh huh! *Told ya!*" to Lucy on this subject, but I suspect she might've caught that vibe from me at some point. It's the small victories that we have to hang on to. I'm still hoping more come along every now and again to keep propelling me forward. However, I won't exactly be holding my breath.

- Score:
  - Bill = 3
  - Lucy = I've lost count